Your Dog
Can Talk

Your Dog Can Talk

A Step-by-Step Guide to Button Training

Christina Hunger, MA, CCC-SLP

TEN SPEED PRESS
California | New York

TEN SPEED PRESS
An imprint of the Crown Publishing Group
A division of Penguin Random House LLC
1745 Broadway
New York, NY 10019
tenspeed.com
penguinrandomhouse.com

Typefaces: Colophon Foundry's Grenette and Milieu Grotesque's Maison Neue

Library of Congress Cataloging-in-Publication Data is on file with the publisher.

ISBN: 978-0-593-83579-1
eBook ISBN: 978-0-593-83580-7

Editor: Cristina Garces
Production editor: Patty Shaw
Designer: Isabelle Gioffredi
Production: Dan Myers
Copy editor: Nancy Inglis
Proofreaders: Robin Slutzky, Sigi Nacson
Publicist: Lauren Chung
Marketer: Allison Renzulli
Illustrations: Jillian Barthold

Manufactured in the United States of America

10 9 8 7 6 5 4 3 2 1

First Edition

The authorized representative in the EU for product safety and compliance is Penguin Random House Ireland, Morrison Chambers, 32 Nassau Street, Dublin D02 YH68, Ireland, https://eu-contact.penguin.ie.

CONTENTS

Your Dog
Can Talk

INTRODUCTION

When I was twenty-four years old, I made a decision in a grocery store parking lot that changed the course of my life and the world forever. I said yes to bringing home Stella, an adorable eight-week-old puppy that my boyfriend and I had fallen in love with.

At the time, I was working as a pediatric speech-language pathologist. Specifically, I helped nonverbal children learn to talk using communication devices. These devices looked like iPads with hundreds of icons, each representing a different word. When the child pressed a button, the device would say the word, allowing the child to express their thoughts, needs, and wants with words for the first time in their lives.

All day, every day, I focused on communication at work. When I came home at night, I couldn't turn this part of my brain off. Within a week of adopting our new puppy, Stella, I had a lightbulb moment: *If dogs can understand the words we say to them, why can't they say words back to us?* I noticed Stella pawing at her water dish when it was empty, gesturing that she needed more. I saw that she was starting to understand the words we were saying to her frequently. I observed Stella barking to get our attention and using different barks for different reasons. I noticed just how many similarities Stella shared with babies and toddlers right before they start talking.

All these observations led me to try something that had never been done before. I decided to see what would happen if I used my skills as a speech therapist with Stella. *Could I teach her to "talk" using a communication device? Could Stella learn to communicate with words if she had a way to say them?* I put my questions to the test, creating a device for her by adapting the technology I used with children and teaching her words in ways similar to how I taught children every day.

Fast-forward to now, just seven years after I programmed my first few buttons for Stella. She has learned to use fifty different words independently. She combines words every day to create her own phrases and short sentences. Stella asks and answers questions, makes comments about what is happening around her, and says how she feels, all thanks to speech therapy.

After my work with Stella became public in 2019, hundreds of thousands of dogs and their humans have followed in Stella's and my footsteps, creating a global talking dog movement. My first book, *How Stella Learned to Talk: The Groundbreaking Story of the World's First Talking Dog,* hit the *New York Times* bestseller list as soon as it was published in 2021, and videos of talking dogs under the hashtag #hunger4words have been viewed over 1 billion times across social media platforms. A study involving thousands of dogs who use buttons to communicate is under way. Research has been published showing that dogs do understand the button words and are creating meaningful, intentional word combinations. I founded the Hunger for Words Talking Pet line of buttons that is sold by major retailers globally, and have spent years working with individual pet parents teaching their own dogs to talk.

Talking dogs are changing the world as we know it. For the first time in history, we have a window into our dogs' minds and can hear firsthand how they're experiencing the environment we share with them. Dogs are using buttons to communicate about concepts that researchers once thought were too advanced for dogs to comprehend, such as time, emotions, and people or places not in their current environment. When we know exactly what our pets need and are thinking about, we can better care for them, strengthen our bond, and create a relationship grounded in mutual respect and communication. When dogs have access to say the words they're understanding, they have agency and autonomy, experience far less frustration from being misunderstood, and become active participants in their lives.

Your Dog Can Talk is the culmination of my years spent studying and practicing speech-language pathology, developing a button communication system for Stella and other dogs to use words, working individually with pet owners, and observing the patterns of thousands of dogs who have used my strategies.

With this book, I invite you to join the talking dog movement to hear what your own dog has to say. The guidance you'll find throughout this book will support you through your entire teaching journey, no matter which stage of learning your pet is in. This guidebook is designed to be a resource you can read and work within as you teach, return to when you have a question or are seeking inspiration, and serve as a keepsake for years to come of your dog's progress.

Part One, "Beginning Learners," will teach you how to recognize your dog's current communication patterns, introduce buttons in the most effective and meaningful ways, and guide you through the exciting first-word milestone. Part Two, "Intermediate Learners," provides expert guidance as you watch your dog blossom into an independent talker, introduce more types of vocabulary, and teach your dog to use words in more complex ways than simply requesting an object or action. Part Three, "Advanced Learners," equips you with everything you need to engage in short conversations with your pet, teach advanced concepts, and work toward becoming a proficient button communicator.

When we believe in our pets' potential to learn and in our own potential to teach, extraordinary things can happen. I'm so excited to support your button communication journey—let's get started!

PART ONE

BEGINNING LEARNERS

Signs Your Dog Is a Beginning Learner

- You haven't introduced buttons yet.
- You've introduced buttons, but your dog hasn't used them.
- Your dog uses between one and six words.
- Your dog uses words, but not every day.
- Your dog needs a lot of help from you to use words.

CHAPTER 1
Why Button Training?

On a Sunday afternoon, my baby woke up from his nap prematurely. After hearing his cries blaring through the monitor, I rushed to his room, took him out of the crib, and bounced him in my arms.

"Sh-sh-sh, it's okay, baby," I said gently.

As I walked around the nursery trying to soothe him back to sleep, I looked out into the hallway to see our dog, Stella, watching intently. Stella sat perfectly still, but her eyes followed my every move.

I wonder what she thinks of all this, I thought. Was she upset that a crying baby interrupted her afternoon nap? Was she waiting for me to be done so I could play with her downstairs? Did she want to come in and lie on the plush rug? Even though I didn't know *what* she was thinking, I knew a fundamental important fact: Stella was thinking *something*.

Despite my best attempts, my baby didn't go back to sleep, continuing to cry on and off for a few more minutes. At some point Stella stood up and trotted down the stairs. I followed as she marched straight to our living room where her board of nearly fifty different buttons is located. Stella uses her buttons every day to express her wants and needs, thoughts, comments, observations, feelings, and questions.

Stella lifted her right paw and pushed down. *Love you,* she said. Head down, she continued walking around her board. I knew that meant she had more to say, so I stayed silent. When Stella reached the other side of her board, she stopped and picked up her paw again. She pushed three buttons in a row to create a phrase: *Bed happy want*. She wanted our baby to be happy in his bedroom, just like I did.

It's moments like these where I feel extreme gratitude for Stella's form of communication, extreme awe of her mind, and extreme connectedness to her. Stella watched me trying to console our upset baby in his room, then walked all the way downstairs to express a message that showed her genuine concern and care.

Without buttons, I would have likely guessed what Stella was thinking and held that assumption as a truth in my mind. I would never have known how much Stella was thinking about our baby and wanting him to be okay. Every assumption we make about our communication partners (human or animal) takes away from an opportunity to learn who they really are. In that moment, through Stella's words, I learned that she was an even more compassionate being than I'd ever imagined.

Button training breaks down the language barrier between humans and their dogs. Communication can now be a true two-way street instead of the human guiding most of the interactions with their pets and speaking on their pet's behalf by guessing what their gestures mean.

What Is Button Training?

Button training is when animals are taught to press buttons programmed to say words in order to communicate their thoughts, wants, and needs.

I developed this form of communication from my experience in the field of speech-language pathology for humans. There are many circumstances in which a person might not be able to communicate with verbal speech, including developmental delays and disorders, accidents, neurodivergence, strokes, and degenerative diseases. When this happens, a speech-language pathologist introduces an augmentative or alternative method of communication, also known as an AAC device. AAC devices are tablets with thousands of different icons, each programmed to say a different word out loud when pressed. AAC devices work because verbal speech is just one form of *expressive language*; there are many other ways to talk!

Other ways to say words include but are not limited to:

- Gesturing
- Typing
- Writing
- Using a communication device (picture Stephen Hawking)

If you've ever lived with a dog, I'm positive there are words that you know your dog understands. Maybe your dog runs to the door every time you say "outside," or jumps around in circles with excitement when you ask, "Wanna go for a walk?" Or maybe you say, "There's a squirrel!" and your dog starts whining and runs to look out the window. These are all examples of your dog's *receptive language* skills, their understanding of language.

According to the American Psychological Association, the average dog understands more than 150 words and has cognitive capabilities close to those of a human child aged two to two and a half. And when we intentionally teach words to dogs, they're capable of understanding *significantly* more than ever expected. The late Dr. John Pilley published a research paper in 2010 showing how he taught his border collie, Chaser, to learn the names of over 1,000 different toys. He also studied Chaser's understanding of word combinations and different syntax patterns. Chaser understood more than just what single words meant; she also understood what they meant when combined together.

Additionally, research in dog cognition over the past decade has consistently shown that brain activity in dogs when they are spoken to matches what brain activity in humans looks like when spoken to. Dogs are likely comprehending much more than we're even aware of. Button communication is a revolutionary system that allows dogs to communicate using the words they're hearing and understanding.

What Are the Benefits of Button Training?

Teaching your dog to talk with buttons brings incredible benefits to both you and your pup.

Buttons Can Help You . . .

Become more observant and understanding

Teaching your dog to talk with buttons requires you to learn about your dog's body language and other forms of communication, observe their communication patterns, and provide patience. While your dog is learning to talk with buttons, you are also learning how to decode all forms of your dog's communication more effectively.

Pet parents often report greater understanding of all their dogs' forms of communication after implementing buttons.

Experience fewer challenging behaviors from your dog (excessive barking or whining, furniture destruction, accidents in the home)

All behavior is communication. When dogs have unmet needs, are misunderstood, or don't have enough mental stimulation, they may resort to harmful behaviors to express themselves or release pent-up energy.

When your dog has the tools to tell you what's on their mind and you're able to understand, their needs can be met quickly. A majority of my training clients who reported these types of challenging behaviors in their dogs noticed a decrease or complete absence of them after their dog learned how to use buttons to talk.

Build an incredible bond with your dog

Solid communication is the foundation of any successful relationship. The more you know about your dog, the more you can appreciate their unique mind and personality and care for them accordingly. Your dog will also appreciate your focus on their communication. The more you try to understand your dog and give them the tools to communicate to their fullest potential, the more likely they'll be to keep communicating with you.

Be amazed every day

Nothing is quite as paradigm-shifting as living with another species who is using words to communicate with you.

In my years of working in this field, I've heard countless stories of how a dog's buttons have impacted their human's lives in unexpected ways. Some pet parents have become vegetarian after realizing the complexities of animals' minds. Others have sought out new career paths in speech-language pathology or animal behavioral sciences. But most consistently, pet parents feel a sense of awe every day when they hear their dog communicating with them.

Buttons Can Help Your Dog . . .

Experience less anxiety and frustration

Anxiety and frustration affect an overwhelming majority of our canine companions. A recent study of over 13,000 dogs showed that nearly 75 percent of all dogs experience anxiety. Dogs may have anxiety related to people, other animals, sounds, and novel situations.

One of the most common behavioral changes pet parents notice after teaching with buttons is reduced anxiety and frustration from their dogs. When we understand our pets, we can help them process situations and provide more support for them when they need it.

Personally, I have also observed significantly less stress and frustration in my dog Stella when we use her buttons to help her cope with changes to her environment. And in the rare occurrence that Stella's buttons aren't available to her, it's shocking to see how much more she whines, barks at me, or paces around.

Have a constant source of mental stimulation

Both physical and mental stimulation contribute to a dog's overall health and well-being. Dogs are cognitive learners who need to use their brains! While puzzle toys and treat dispensers for dogs are certainly fun, the effects of most of these mental stimulation products are short lived. Your dog learns how to get the food out, and the experience is over for them in a matter of minutes.

Buttons provide an incredible amount of mental stimulation. It takes mental focus and energy for your dog to process what's happening, think about what they want to say and find the corresponding buttons. Even when a word is learned, your dog can continue using it in new ways and in more complex situations (which you'll learn all about through this guidebook).

Be understood no matter who is caring for them

Every dog has their own unique tendencies and communication patterns. So much of understanding a dog's whines or barks comes from background knowledge of their typical routines and behaviors, which a dog sitter may not have.

For example, my dog Stella often whines in the living room when she wants to look out the window. If she was whining, a sitter would not likely jump to that conclusion. But if Stella used her buttons to say *want look outside,* the sitter could know to open the blinds and let her look out the window.

Buttons allow your dog to communicate their wants and needs, and be understood, even when you're gone.

Have greater autonomy

Humans make most of the decisions in a dog's life. We're in charge of the food they eat, where they go, what they play with, who they see, when they go for walks, and what type of training or other activities they participate in. Providing dogs with more choices throughout their days improves their emotional well-being and decreases their stress levels.

Button communication can give dogs the ability to have more control over their environment and be an active participant in their daily lives. Instead of having their humans make most of their decisions for them, dogs who use buttons can express exactly where they want to go, who they want to see, or what they want to be doing.

How Does Button Training Differ from Traditional Dog Training?

Both dog training and button training are valuable in their own ways. Dog training helps dogs learn the right behaviors to function well in society and to keep them safe. Button training gives dogs a way to express their thoughts, wants, and needs to their humans. Button training is meant to teach your dog *language.*

There may be some similarities or overlap in a few areas, but button communication is far more similar to teaching a baby or toddler to talk. If you're a parent of young children, many of the strategies throughout this guidebook can be used with toddlers, too! Dogs are incredible learners. When we give them the opportunity to learn in a manner similar to children, we can be amazed by what dogs are capable of achieving.

WHAT BUTTON TRAINING IS	WHAT BUTTON TRAINING ISN'T
Teaching to use words for communication	Training to push a button
Teaching to use buttons independently	Training to "say" specific words on command
Responding to your pet's message	Rewarding behaviors with treats
A skill that takes time to develop	An instant solution
An additional tool for communication	The only way a pet will communicate
Your pet's voice	A party trick

What Is the Hunger for Words Method?

When teaching your dog to talk, the buttons and the methodology are equally as important. The buttons are the *tool* your dog needs to be able to say words, and the methodology is the *information* that you need in order to teach your dog how to communicate with words. The Hunger for Words Method is a systematic approach to teaching dogs to communicate with buttons derived from research in augmentative communication, early language development, and dog cognition. The four core components of the Hunger for Words Method are as follows:

Four Core Components

1. Variety of Vocabulary

Dogs need to have buttons that represent different concepts in order to learn that each button serves a unique purpose. When dogs are introduced to a variety of words, they learn that buttons are a tool they can use to communicate about a variety of topics.

2. Modeling

Dogs learn how to use buttons intentionally and independently by watching how you use them. The more exposure your dog has to buttons, the more they'll be able to learn what they're for.

3. Responding (Meaningful Responses)

Dogs learn the meaning and power of each word by seeing how their caregivers respond to it, or how the environment around them changes.

4. Muscle Memory

Dogs need their buttons to stay in consistent locations to develop muscle memory for each word. When muscle memory is established, dogs can find and use their words with ease.

These four core components provide a framework for all of the teaching strategies, recommendations and advice throughout each stage of learning. When you use these four core components to guide your teaching, your dog can learn to use words independently and become a proficient button communicator.

Frequently Asked Questions

As you're preparing to start teaching your pet to talk, you may have a few questions.

Can older dogs learn to talk? Or do you have to start teaching dogs from puppyhood?

Dogs of all ages have the potential to learn! Over the past few years I've seen dogs throughout their lifespan learn to use words. Sometimes older dogs actually learn faster than puppies because they already understand what many different words mean. You may be surprised by your dog's capabilities!

Is button communication only for certain breeds of dogs?

While certain breeds and personalities of dogs may be more talkative than others (just like different personalities of humans), all dog breeds have the potential to learn.

Will I have to say yes to everything my dog asks for?

This is a common concern pet parents have before programming their first buttons! No, I promise you will not have to say yes every time your dog asks for something. Throughout this guidebook, you'll learn how to respond to requests even if you can't provide the activity, and why it's important to give your dog a voice even if you can't always say yes.

Activities

Now that you understand what button communication is, it's time to get started! Before we dive into learning your dog's language in the next chapter, spend a few minutes on the activities below. It will be so fun for you to look back at your activities from each chapter and have a record of your communication journey with your pet for years to come.

1. Find Your Why

As you're beginning your button communication journey with your pet, take a few moments to reflect on *why* you want to teach your pet to talk. Were you inspired by pets you've seen online? Do you want to know what your dog is trying to say when they're whining at you? Do you want to give your dog a way to communicate their basic needs? Do you want to build a relationship founded in mutual communication?

Fill in the blank here to create your why statement(s).

I'm teaching [pet's name] to talk because _____

_____

_____

_____

_____.

These statements will serve as your guideposts throughout your teaching journey. When you need inspiration or are wondering how to move forward, come back to your why to help you decide what to do.

2. Set Your Goals

With your whys in mind, take a few more moments to create your top two goals for your button communication journey. Maybe you have introduced a few words and are looking to expand your pet's vocabulary. Maybe you have a service dog with whom you want to communicate more effectively. Or maybe you want to better understand the dog you just adopted from a shelter. Whatever your top goals are, write them down so you remember what you're striving for as you're teaching.

As an example, I'll share the top two goals I had for Stella when she first began to use button communication, and how they shaped my teaching:

Stella will be able to express her wants and needs regardless of who is caring for her. This meant I always wanted Stella to be taken care of and for her to be able to advocate for herself. With this goal in mind, I focused on generalizing her vocabulary with different people and in different environments to promote her independence.

Stella will be able to communicate about the parts of her day that are most important to her, and about the environment we share. This meant that I wanted to give Stella the opportunity to share her thoughts about the people, places, activities, and routines she encountered throughout her day. With this goal in mind, I selected vocabulary applicable to her routines and activities, and prioritized teaching throughout those events.

Your turn!

MY TOP TWO GOALS FOR [PET'S NAME]

1 _____

_____

2 _____

_____

Great work! Teaching with intention will help set you and your pet up for success.

CHAPTER 2

Learning Your Dog's Language

One evening after we returned home from a trip to the dog beach, Stella walked inside, then sat in front of the door and whined at me. I assumed she wanted to go back outside and return to the beach.

"All done outside, Stella," I said. "Time to eat. Eat now."

Stella didn't budge. She looked at me, sighed, then pawed at the door.

"Sorry, girl. All done outside." I walked into the kitchen to start preparing our dinner.

After about thirty seconds, Stella walked to her button board and said, *Toy inside*. She returned to her post in front of the door and stared at me one more time.

Then it clicked. After I had washed Stella off, I forgot to grab her toy and bring it back inside with us. Sure enough, when I opened the door, Stella pounced on her toy, shook it in her mouth, and trotted back in, where she continued playing.

All parts of this exchange were equally important. Gestures provided the foundation for communication. If Stella had said, *Toy inside,* without standing near the door, I would have assumed she wanted to play with one of her toys inside. I probably would have pulled a few options out of her basket and tried to engage with her, which wouldn't have been what she was wanting, either.

Words add more specificity and complexity. I was partially right about her nonverbal communication. The standing by the door, sighing, and pawing at the door did all mean that she wanted to go outside. But the words added the why. Without words, Stella wouldn't have had a way to tell me exactly what she was trying to express in that moment. Without the why, I denied her request because I didn't understand it.

Teaching your dog to use words does not replace their gestures; it builds on them. Through this chapter, you'll learn how important your dog's body language is, how you can find your dog's current communication patterns, and how you can use these patterns to your advantage as you begin your button communication journey.

The Importance of Gestures, Sounds, and Body Language

Communication is much more than words, even for humans. Waving hi to your neighbor, shaking your head no at your partner, or shrugging your shoulders in uncertainty to your friend are all valid and meaningful expressions of communication.

Before you can teach your dog to use words, it's important to learn and decode their current communication patterns and natural body language. When I worked as a speech therapist, this was the starting point in treatment plans with children, too. Babies and toddlers communicate via gestures and body language *before* they are able to say a word for a concept. Research shows that a child's gestures correlate to the verbal words that develop later. For example, a baby will likely wave bye before being able to say the word *bye,* or will smack their lips together when hungry before being able to say that they want food. Gestures provide insight into what a learner is understanding and communicating, and which words are likely developing soon.

Dogs naturally express themselves extremely well using gestures, vocalizations, and body language. This provides an excellent foundation for learning to use words because they are already demonstrating symbolic communication. A gesture symbolizes a thought, feeling, or desire that they are sharing with you. By observing your dog's current communication patterns, you can learn which concepts they naturally communicate about, begin consistently responding to their communication, and make informed decisions about which words to introduce first.

This represents a *strengths-based approach* to teaching. When we focus on our dogs' communication strengths and natural inclinations, we can teach words and concepts they would be excited to say and see faster progress than if we tried to begin with their deficits. Communication is about connection. So the best place to start is finding the times when your dog is already trying to connect with you. Let's get started!

Common Forms of Canine Communication

Dogs are complex, intelligent creatures who are incredibly expressive. When you know what to look for, you'll be amazed at how much information your pup is communicating to you on a daily basis. I've grouped common canine communication patterns into three categories—vocalizations, gestures, and body language—along with what they typically indicate. Each form of communication may have a different meaning depending on the context and other accompanying cues.

Take a look at the list below and circle or star the forms of expression you recognize your dog exhibiting.

VOCALIZATIONS

Whining: Expressing a desire for an object, an action, some attention from a caregiver, or some other need. Use context clues to decode the desire.
Barking: Dogs have different barks for different communicative functions. Dogs may bark to protect themselves or their owners, express fear or anxiety, initiate play, express excitement, call out to their owner, respond to another dog's barks, or express a desire for an object, an action, or some attention from their caregiver.
Howling: Calling out to other dogs or their owners, responding to other dogs' vocalizations, expressing anxiety.
Huffing / Sighing: Expressing frustration / discontentment.

GESTURES

Pawing: Desiring something to happen with the object (for example, pawing at a water dish when it's empty, pawing the door when wanting to go outside, pawing your hand when wanting scratches).
Cocking head to the side: Expressing curiosity or interest in an object, activity, or word.
Joint attention via eye contact: looking at an object, location, or person, then looking back at you: Directing your attention toward the object they're

looking at. This could indicate needing help (for example, looking at the toy under the chair, then looking to you), expressing excitement (for example, looking toward the friend at the door, then looking at you and wagging tail).

Positioning: Dogs will often sit or stand near a desired object or activity.

BODY LANGUAGE

Tail wagging: An excited or aroused state.

Tail tucked: Showing nervousness, stress, or apprehension.

Ears back: Can indicate a relaxed, happy state or a fearful state depending on the context and other cues.

Ears perked: Indicates a highly aroused state.

Bowing: An invitation to play.

Finding Your Dog's Current Communication Patterns

Using the characteristics above as a reference point, complete the following chart to begin identifying your pet's current communication patterns. You can use my example below as a guide.

A note on puppies or dogs who are new to you: If you are in the beginning of your relationship with your pet, you may not know the answers to these prompts. That's okay! Spend a few days observing your dog's behavior and jotting down notes here as you observe them.

Example:

PROMPT	RESPONSE	DOMINANT FORM(S) OF COMMUNICATION
I know my dog needs to go outside when . . .	*They stand near the door and whine*	*Positioning Whining*
My dog shows me they're ready to eat by . . .	*Pawing their food dish*	*Pawing*
I know my dog wants to go for a walk when . . .	*They turn their head when I say "walk," then wag their tail*	*Cocking head Wagging tail*
If my dog needs help with something, they usually . . .	*Bark at me and stand near where they need help*	*Positioning Barking*
My dog wants my attention most when . . .	*I'm working or on the phone*	*Whining*

PROMPT	RESPONSE	DOMINANT FORM(S) OF COMMUNICATION
I know my dog wants to play when . . .	They bring me a toy	Joint attention
I can tell my dog is upset when . . .	They sigh or huff at me when I say no	Sighing / huffing
I can tell my dog is happy when . . .	They wag their tail, smile, and wiggle	Tail wagging
My dog shows they want affection when . . .	They fold their body in front of me and move where they want to be petted	Positioning
I feel most confused about what my dog is trying to tell me when . . .	They whine at me, but don't need to go out and have already been fed	Whining

Your turn!

PROMPT	RESPONSE	DOMINANT FORM(S) OF COMMUNICATION
I know my dog needs to go outside when . . .		
My dog shows me she's ready to eat by . . .		
I know my dog wants to go for a walk when . . .		
If my dog needs help with something, she usually . . .		
My dog wants my attention most when . . .		
I know my dog wants to play when . . .		
I can tell my dog is upset when . . .		
I can tell my dog is happy when . . .		
My dog shows she wants affection when . . .		
I feel most confused about what my dog is trying to tell me when . . .		

How to Use This Information

Take a look at your "dominant form(s) of communication" column. Are there several different forms, or just a couple of primary ways your dog expresses themself?

Tally up your answers, and write down your results here:

FORM OF COMMUNICATION	NUMBER OF TIMES
Whining	
Barking	
Howling	
Sighing / huffing	
Pawing	
Cocking head to side	
Joint attention via eye contact	
Positioning	
Tail wagging	
Tail tucked	
Ears back	
Ears perked	
Bowing	

Top Three Forms of Communication

1 _____

2 _____

3 _____

Your communication chart can show you valuable insights about both you and your dog. Was this chart easy or difficult to complete? If it was easy, you probably have a solid understanding of how your dog is expressing themself. This is a great foundation to begin from. If it was more challenging to fill in, don't worry! In the activities below, you'll learn how to be a communication detective and look for more patterns throughout your days together. We'll use the information from our charts to guide us as we move through the next few chapters.

Activities

1. Become a Communication Detective

Take a look at your dog's top three forms of communication. Now that you've identified them and know what to look for, spend a couple of days as an observer. See if you can find other situations where your dog is communicating to you that you might not have realized before. You might even notice new forms of communication!

If you have a new dog or you weren't yet sure how to answer the prompts above, familiarize yourself with the "Common Forms of Canine Communication" section on page 21. Watch your dog go about their day with these characteristics in mind. When you spot one, jot it down here so you remember what they did and the context. You can use your notes to complete the chart above, too.

Write down your discoveries below.

Example:

I realized that my dog huffs when I'm not able to take her outside right away.

I REALIZED THAT . . .

My dog _____ when _____.

My dog _____ when _____.

My dog _____ when _____.

My dog _____ when _____.

My dog _____ when _____.

2. Operation Narration

By now you should have a solid understanding of at least a few ways and times of day your dog consistently communicates to you. Start narrating your dog's actions and desires with short, simple phrases. Both humans and dogs have to hear words *a lot* before being able to use words. The more you talk to your dog about what's happening and pair words with her nonverbal communication, the easier it will be for her to learn the meaning of different words.

EXAMPLES

If your dog paws at the door to go outside, you can say, "Want outside? Outside. Okay, let's go outside," all before opening the door.

As your dog bows and pounces on a toy, you could say, "Playtime! Let's play! Yes, play, play, play," while engaging in play together.

When your dog stands near her food bowl and whines, you can say "Ready to eat? Time to eat. Eat, eat, eat," as you're preparing her food.

If your dog barks at you for attention while you're reading, you could put your book down, look at your dog, and say, "Look, look, look. I'm looking. Mom look."

Summary

Learning your dog's natural forms of communication is a crucial first step in teaching words. Gestures, vocalizations, and body language serve as an excellent foundation to build from. As you listen and respond to your dog now, you are establishing a solid relationship together grounded in mutual respect and two-way communication. By labeling your dog's nonverbal communication with words, you are beginning to teach the meaning of words to your pup.

CHAPTER 3

Selecting Beginning Words

When I was working as a speech therapist, a child was transferred over to my caseload who was labeled as "not suitable for AAC." This young boy was only three years old, had autism spectrum disorder, and had never said a word with verbal speech. The clinician who worked with him previously tried teaching him to press a single button programmed to say *more* for five months with no success. The boy's parents thought he couldn't learn, the boy's other therapists had given up on trying to teach him other skills, and the boy started becoming more and more upset each time he arrived for therapy.

When we started working together, I took a different approach. Instead of waiting for him to master one word before teaching others, I gave him much more vocabulary from the start. During every activity we did together, we had options for words we could use to talk about what was happening. Because there were so many words available, this boy saw me using his device *constantly*.

Within a short few weeks of this change, the boy's communication and participation completely took off. He started using five to ten different words on his own immediately, became excited by therapy, and eventually went on to start combining words together on his own and talking *constantly*.

When I first introduced buttons to Stella, I made a mistake similar to that of the clinician who worked with the boy before me. Since potty training was our most pressing need at the time, I programmed one single button to say *outside.* For a couple of weeks, we made absolutely no progress, and I briefly considered that Stella was not capable of learning this skill. But then I thought back to the boy at work and quickly realized that I needed to add more buttons. If we had more buttons available to Stella, she would see me using them much more frequently throughout the day and would have options of what to say.

A few weeks after I made this switch in our home, Stella became much more interested in the buttons and went on to start using them on her own. Now, after years of working with other pet parents and their dogs, I've seen the same patterns over and over again. Dogs have a much greater chance of learning how to communicate with buttons when they have more than one button to begin with.

The advice in this chapter will help you figure out the correct number of words to start with and the best types of words to get your dog talking.

Number of Words

I typically recommend starting with four to six words. This is a manageable number for both you and your dog, optimum for providing you with opportunities to teach different concepts throughout your day without the process becoming overwhelming for either of you.

If you know you want to have a larger vocabulary available for your dog, you can start with up to ten to twelve words. Starting with more buttons can give your dog more options and can empower them to use words in different scenarios from the beginning. If you have a background in working with communication devices, have more time to dedicate to button training, or live with family members who are on board, too, starting with a larger vocabulary set might be the right choice for you.

Types of Words

Vocabulary selection is one of the most important aspects of teaching your dog to talk. Since your dog will be able to say only the words that you give them access to, your selections hold significant weight. The first words you teach are especially important, as they introduce your pet to the concept of using buttons to communicate and lay the foundation for all that's to come.

In the world of augmentative communication, there are two main groups of words: *core words* and *fringe words*.

Core words can be defined as "a small set of simple words that are used frequently and across contexts." Core words are typically verbs, adjectives, prepositions, conjunctions, and pronouns, and make up the majority of the language we use when we speak. The average adult human knows approximately 40,000 words, yet the same 500 core words account for nearly 80 percent of what we say.

The remaining 20 percent of words we use on a daily basis are called fringe words. Fringe words can be defined as "words specific to a topic, individual, or environment." Fringe words are mostly nouns and proper nouns.

Let's take a look at four pairs of similar words and determine which is the core word and which is the fringe word.

TOPIC	OPTION 1	OPTION 2	ANALYSIS
Playtime	*Play*	*Ball*	*Play* is the core word and *ball* is the fringe word here. *Play* can be used to talk about all types of play, whereas *ball* can be used only to talk about ball play.
Going outside	*Outside*	*Walk*	*Outside* is the core word and *walk* is the fringe word here. *Outside* can be used to talk about all trips outside: taking bathroom breaks, playing in the yard, walking, going to the park, whereas *walk* is specific to one activity.
Eating	*Eat*	*Treat*	*Eat* is the core word and *treat* is the fringe word here. *Eat* can be used to talk about eating breakfast, dinner, treats, and even your own mealtime, whereas *treat* is specific to one type of food.
Drinking	*Water*	*Drink*	This is a tricky one. In this case, *water* is the core word and *drink* is the fringe word. For dogs, we can use *water* to talk about filling up their water bowl, the rain outside, playing in water, and more. *Drink* would be used only to talk about filling up their water bowl.

We all need both core words and fringe words to communicate effectively. When setting up your dog's vocabulary, I recommend striving for the

80/20 balance between core and fringe words. This ratio doesn't have to be exact, but core words should make up most of your buttons, especially in the beginning. You can add fringe words down the road to give your dog more specificity in their communication.

Characteristics of First Words

At the beginning of their button communication journey, your dog will likely say words to make requests. This means they'll use their buttons to tell you what they want or need. As your dog's skills progress, they'll use words for many more reasons. We'll learn about all of those in the intermediate and advanced parts of this guidebook. For now, focus on words that allow your dog to tell you what they need or want.

A great beginning vocabulary set consists of words that . . .

You Naturally Say to Your Dog

Your dog has been hearing and learning the words you say on a daily basis ever since you brought them home. Matching your dog's buttons to your vocabulary patterns will help set them up for success.

Your Dog Already Understands

Both humans and dogs have to understand words before we can use them appropriately. We all have those words that we have to spell out or else our dogs go crazy! Which words does your dog react strongly to? These are the words you know they understand.

Come Up Frequently Throughout Your Days

The more you can model words for your dog, the faster they will be able to learn what the words mean and how they can use them. Modeling means using your dog's buttons as you're talking to your dog. You'll learn all about this strategy in chapter 5 (page 49). Choose words that you can envision yourself using on a daily basis.

Are Motivating or Exciting to Your Dog

We all communicate most about the things we love, dogs included! Make sure to pick words that your dog would want to say.

Are Easy for You to Teach and Respond To

Responding to what your dog says is very important in the early stages of teaching with buttons. Make it easier on yourself by picking words that are easy to respond to. For example, if your dog says *come*, you can easily move over to them to reinforce the meaning. But if your dog says the name of a beloved friend, you probably can't easily make that friend appear. Save those words for later when your dog already has a grasp on button communication and doesn't need the immediate reinforcement.

Represent Concepts Your Dog Already Communicates About

As we learned in chapter 2, gestures for a concept come before words in typical language development. If your dog already stands near the door to show they need to go outside or paws at their water dish to let you know it's empty, these are great words to start with.

Putting It All Together

With the above characteristics in mind, take a look at the charts below. Circle the words from each table that seem most relevant to you and your pet.

POPULAR BEGINNING CORE WORDS	WHY THEY WORK
Outside	All dogs need to go outside, and all pet parents need to know when their pet wants and needs to go! Going outside is both functional and important. It occurs multiple times per day.
Play	Playing is natural for dogs. They play independently, with their humans, and with other animals. *Play* can be applied to all types of play, and most pups play frequently.
Eat	Dogs are excellent at learning through routine activities. Eating is something that happens every day and is often very motivating.
Water	Dogs drink water every day, and can also generalize the concept to talk about playing in the rain, swimming, taking a bath, and more.
Love You	We give our dogs affection, and our dogs give us affection. *Love you* gives your dog a way to communicate about these times and express their desire for more connection.

POPULAR BEGINNING CORE WORDS	WHY THEY WORK
All done	For every activity we start, we also finish. You can use *all done* to narrate when your dog is all done outside, eating, playing, drinking water, etc.
Bye	Leaving the home with and without our dogs happens daily. This gives your pup the opportunity to talk about these events.
Come	Think about how many times we tell our dogs to *come*. You can model this word whenever you're naturally calling your dog over, and when your dog is wanting you to move to them.

POPULAR BEGINNING FRINGE WORDS	WHY THEY WORK
Walk	Walks are highly motivating and often a staple routine in dogs' days. Give your pup the ability to ask for what they want instead of waiting all day for you to say it.
Bed	Bedtime occurs every day, which provides a great, consistent teaching opportunity. Dogs often learn to narrate their sequences of events, going to bed or waking up included!
Bone	If your dog receives bones on a regular basis, you can turn this routine into a language-teaching activity.
Treat	If your dog receives treats on a regular basis, you can turn this routine into a language-teaching activity.
Ball	If your dog has a highly preferred way of playing or specific toy name you use frequently, this can be a great supplemental choice.
Toy (or specific toy name)	If your dog has a highly preferred way of playing or specific toy name you use frequently, this can be a great supplemental choice.
Daycare or Park	If your dog's routine involves going to a daycare or park multiple times a week, this can be a great supplemental word to discuss this activity.
Scratches	If your dog loves one specific form of affection, like getting scratches, this could be a good supplemental choice.

Activities

1. First Words Formula

Complete the three steps below to select your beginning vocabulary set.

1 Decide how many buttons you want to start with.

2 Review the core words and fringe words you have circled above and narrow down your selections. If you have brainstormed other ideas not on the lists, that's great, too! Use this table to help you select the number of core vs. fringe words to choose.

TOTAL NUMBER OF STARTING WORDS	TARGET NUMBER OF CORE WORDS	TARGET NUMBER OF FRINGE WORDS
4	3–4	0–1
6	5–6	0–1
8	6–8	1–2
10	7–8	2–3
12	9–10	2–3

3 Ask yourself the following questions. When you can answer yes to all of these, you are ready to go!

- *Are these words that I naturally say or plan to say to my dog?* If they aren't, adjust by thinking of what you normally say during that topic. Here's an example. You have selected *eat,* but you only ever say *hungry* to your pup. Swap in your preferred word.
- *Do they represent a variety of topics / concepts throughout the day?* If not, take out one of the fringe words you have for a topic and substitute a core word for a new topic. Here's an example. Suppose you've selected *outside, park, walk,* and *eat.* Remove *park* or *walk* and add a new core word that's unrelated to going outside. You can use *outside* to talk about all or most outside trips in the beginning.
- *If my dog says these words, would I be able to respond most of the time?* If not, try removing a word that takes place outside of your home and swap it with a word that takes place in your home. Remember, eventually you will be able to say no, but for the introductory period we want to be enthusiastic and consistent in our responses.

2. Write Down Your Final Selections

WORD NO.	SELECTION
1	
2	
3	
4	
5	
6	
7	
8	
9	
10	
11	
12	

FREQUENTLY ASKED QUESTIONS ABOUT BEGINNING WORDS

Why shouldn't I start with just one button? Wouldn't it be less confusing for my dog to introduce one word at a time?

I recommend starting with more than one word for two reasons.

First, your dog will learn what the buttons are for and what they mean by seeing you use them throughout the day. If you have only one button available, this automatically means that your dog will only see the buttons in use a maximum of a few times each day. Imagine that you start with only an *outside* button. You take your dog out three times each day and model "outside" before each trip. This means your dog would see a button in use only three times each day. Now imagine you have buttons for *outside, play, eat, water, walk, love you.* You model each relevant word before going outside, playing with your dog, feeding them, filling up their water bowl, taking them for a walk, and giving them belly rubs and scratches. This means your dog would see the buttons in use probably about ten times each day. That makes a huge difference!

Second, it can be more difficult for your dog to learn that each button has a different meaning if they only have one button to begin with. Beginning with more than one word teaches your dog from the start that each button represents a different word and serves a unique purpose. You won't have to worry about your dog using every button to mean the same thing when you begin with more than one from the start.

Is it okay to give my dog a *treat* button? I'm afraid they'll just ask for treats all day long.

Instead of starting with *treat*, I recommend starting with a core word like *eat*. You can model *eat* when you're giving your pup each of her meals, when you give her treats, when you're eating your own meals, and when you give her any toys that include treats. Whatever you decide to do, make sure to stay away from beginning with only a *treat* button and no other words. It can be very challenging for your pup to unlearn that buttons lead to treats. Don't give your dog a treat for saying a word unless the word is food-related. This confuses the meaning of the button for your dog.

If you're worried about your dog asking for food all day, I encourage you to think about all the other activities your dog enjoys and already communicates about. Do they love getting belly rubs, playing, snuggling on the couch with you, going for walks? Yes, food is motivating for many dogs, but so are lots of other activities! You can always say no to more food requests, especially once they learn the meaning of the word. We will talk more about this in the coming chapters.

I want my dog to be able to tell me when she's in pain or when something is wrong. Can I introduce these concepts in the beginning?

I completely understand wanting to know when your pet is not feeling well. But in your early days of button training, you'll want to pick concepts that are easy for you to teach on a daily basis and that are easy for you to respond to. Get your dog accustomed to the concept of button communication first, then add more complex concepts later on. We'll cover these topics in Parts Two and Three.

Summary

Selecting a solid vocabulary set is an essential part of teaching your dog to talk with buttons. Understanding what makes a good word choice will help you continue to choose new words for your dog along your journey. Refer back to this chapter whenever you need a refresher on the different types of vocabulary. Now that you have your first words picked out, move on to chapter 4 to figure out the best way to set up your buttons. You'll be teaching your pup in no time!

CHAPTER 4
Setting Up Your Buttons

One of the questions I'm asked most frequently is how Stella knows what each button means.

Ever since I started sharing videos of Stella using her buttons to talk, viewers have speculated about whether Stella is distinguishing the colors of each button or reading the labels below the words. They even surmise that I have coated each button with a unique scent. The truth is much simpler: location, location, location! Dogs memorize the location of each word.

One of my earliest memories of a dog learning the locations of objects involved our family dog, Wrigley, while I was growing up. I remember when we moved her food and water dishes to the mudroom instead of the kitchen, it took time for her to adjust. Even though she was standing near her dishes in the mudroom, when we said, "Do you want to eat?" she would cock her head and run to the space in the kitchen where her dishes used to be. It took her a couple of weeks to adjust and start running to the new location consistently. The same thing happened when we moved her kennel into a new room. For the first couple of weeks after we switched the location, she would run to her kennel's previous site every time she saw us getting ready to leave the house.

Motor Memory

When I was in graduate school learning about communication devices, I finally understood the science behind what was happening with Wrigley all those years ago. Wrigley had built a motor plan (also known as a muscle memory) for where each of her objects was located. The association was so strong between activities and their locations that it took a couple of weeks for her brain to form a completely new association and be able to respond automatically.

Watching Wrigley learn the new location was fascinating, as it didn't just click in one day; it came in stages. First, Wrigley ran to the old spot. Next, she followed our cues as we pointed in the direction of the new location or walked toward it. Then Wrigley would pause and think before running. And finally she ran instinctively to the new home for her dishes or her kennel.

What I didn't know at the time was that Wrigley was moving through the three stages of motor learning (shown below), which is the same process human AAC users go through when learning the locations of words on their devices, and the same process we all go through to learn things like tying our shoes, typing, and opening apps on our smartphones.

STAGE	FORMAL NAME	CHARACTERISTICS
1	Cognitive	• Learner is exploring • Learner does not understand what they're doing wrong when mistakes happen • Learner needs assistance
2	Associative	• Learner is refining their skill • Learner makes some errors, but is able to self-correct • Learner can perform with undivided attention
3	Automatic	• "Conscious thought is no longer needed" • Learner can perform independently and while multitasking • Errors rarely occur

Dogs progress through these three stages when learning how to use their buttons, too. Dogs are able to reach the third stage when their buttons are kept in consistent locations and they are given lots of opportunities to practice. Because of this, the most important factor when setting up your dog's buttons is always keeping them in the same order. When you choose a spot for a word, keep it there.

Where to Set Up Buttons

Now that we know how important it is to keep your dog's buttons in their designated spots, it's time to figure out the best placement in your home for both you and your dog.

Option 1: Buttons Around the Home

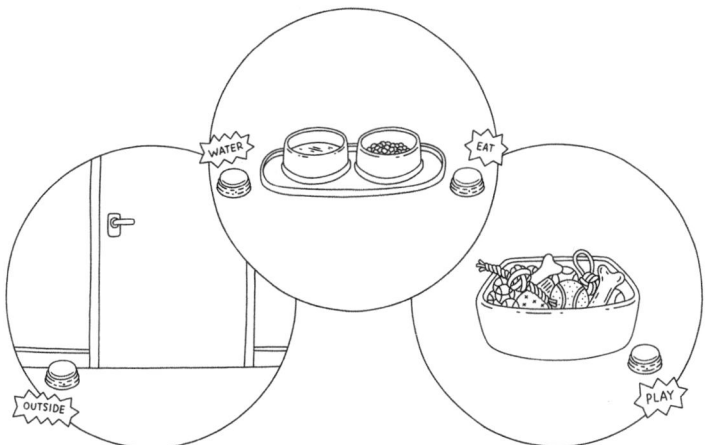

The first option for setting up your buttons is placing each word near its respective activity. This would mean placing *outside* near the door, *eat* near your dog's food dish, *play* near toys, etc.

This setup works best for young puppies who live in larger homes. Puppies have fleeting attention spans, so keeping buttons as close to their meanings as possible can help them learn. This is especially important when it comes to potty training. When a puppy lets you know they have to go to the bathroom, there is a very short window of time before they go. Keeping your *outside* button near the door can help reduce the number of accidents that happen on the way to the door. (If you have a puppy and live in a smaller space where you're within steps of the door, food, toys, etc., then you can move on to option two.)

Option 1 also works well if you know from the start that you want to keep a more limited vocabulary for your dog. If you do not want an expansive vocabulary of more than ten words eventually, you can easily keep your dog's buttons throughout your home.

Option 2: Buttons in One Central Location

The second option for setting up your buttons is finding one central location in your home to keep them. You can place the buttons in a mat that keeps them organized, secured, and always in the same order. This setup works well for dogs who live in smaller spaces, humans who want to expand their pet's vocabulary throughout their lifespan, dogs who are already housebroken, and dogs with longer attention spans than young puppies.

Keeping buttons in one central location is beneficial for long-term growth because dogs can much more easily combine words together when all their words are in the same area of the house. With the use of a button mat, you can add new words without changing the locations of buttons, too.

Keeping buttons in one central location on a mat also works well if you travel with your dog or want to be able to move your buttons to different areas of your home. If you move the entire mat with the buttons inside, your dog's words will always stay in the same order, which will enable them to communicate without needing time to relearn where each button is in a new environment.

Best Areas of the Home for Your Buttons

Your dog will have the best chance to learn how to use their buttons if these are easily accessible to them and are modeled frequently by you. In order for this to happen, your buttons should be somewhere that:

- You and your dog naturally spend time together
- Is near a majority of your dog's favorite activities
- Is highly visible to remind you to model words
- Is audible from most rooms on the same floor

Depending on their floor plan, most pet parents choose to place their buttons in their living room, in their kitchen, or in larger entryways. Once you've picked your room, take a look at this second list of criteria to make sure your placement is optimized. Buttons should be located:

- Somewhere free of clutter
- Away from the wall or other furniture to begin. This will give your dog the opportunity to approach the buttons from multiple angles, however is most comfortable for them.
- In a space large enough to accommodate more buttons next to or below your buttons in the future

Frequently Asked Questions About Button Setup

What should I do if I live in a small apartment? I want my dog to be able to use words, but I don't have the space!

It's completely possible for your dog to communicate a majority of their wants, needs, thoughts, and ideas with a smaller vocabulary that will not take up a lot of space. When you're selecting words, choose words that are more general that can be used in multiple different situations and contexts. Verbs and adjectives will give you more flexibility than nouns. By using button mats, you can still have up to twelve buttons in a space that's only about two feet long.

What should I do if I live in a larger home with multiple levels? I won't always be near my dog's buttons if they're downstairs in the living room.

Each type of home comes with its own benefits and challenges for button setup. Smaller homes have less room for expansion, but larger homes mean you're not near the buttons all the time. I recommend setting your buttons up in a button mat so that you can bring your buttons to another area of your home if you know you and your dog will be spending a lot of time there.

43

For example, you can keep your buttons' home base in the living room. If you work from your home office on the second floor and your dog hangs out near you for most of the day, you can take the mat up with you. The buttons will stay in the same order and your dog will have access to them during your working hours.

If I have multiple dogs, do I need separate sets of buttons for each of them?

No, not necessarily. In all of the multi-dog homes I've worked with, the dogs have shared their buttons. Most often, one dog will learn to use them quicker than the other(s), and the other(s) will follow that dog's lead.

Do I need to place all related words together on the same mat? For example, should I plan to place the *play* button next to words like *park* or *ball*?

No, this is not necessary. I recommend keeping all of your dog's essential words on one to two mats so that you can always remove them and travel with a smaller setup if needed. This strategy mimics the way human AAC devices are set up. A person's core words are on the front screen, and more specific fringe vocabulary can be found on subsequent pages. This enables the AAC user to communicate the majority of their messages with the most ease, and still be able to talk throughout their days if only the first screen is available to them.

Try not to overthink the individual locations for your buttons. The most important factor is keeping words in a consistent placement so your dog can develop a motor plan.

I started with buttons around my home. When should I move them all to a mat?

If you began teaching your dog to talk by placing buttons around your home near their respective activities, you may need to change your setup as your dog's skills progress. Keeping your buttons in one central location allows for your dog to combine words and use words for multiple meanings easily.

Timing is everything when transitioning your setup. The best time to transition your buttons to one central location is when:

Your dog uses multiple buttons independently every day

Your dog will be more likely to learn the new button locations if buttons are important to them. It will also be easier for them to relearn just a location than to learn how to use buttons independently and in a new spot at the same time.

Your dog's vocabulary has grown to ten plus words

If your dog has this many words available, it can be difficult to remember to model them all when they're scattered throughout your home. Keeping your buttons in the area where you spend the most time will help your dog learn to use words for different purposes.

Your dog has begun combining words or using words in unique ways

Right before dogs start combining words together intentionally, they typically use words in new ways or for different purposes. If you see that your dog is combining words, you'll know it's time to bring your buttons together. This will enable your dog to continue progressing and sharing the more complex thoughts on their mind.

What should I do if I need to switch my dog's setup?

When you've determined that it's the right time to transition your buttons to one central location, follow these steps:

1 **Plan your new setup.** Before moving buttons around, purchase your mats and get them ready. Choose a new place in your home to keep your buttons (see page 41, for location guidance).

2 **Place the buttons in your mats.** Keep any patterns consistent with your former setup. If you had any buttons near each other when they were scattered throughout your home, keep them near each other on the mats as well.

3 **Model all your dog's buttons.** Take time to call your dog over and show them where their words are now. Model them all a few times in a row.

4 **Increase your modeling.** A new setup takes time to learn. Model words as if you are introducing them for the first time. Increase your repetitions. The more your dog sees you using buttons in the new locations, the easier time they'll have learning.

5 **Give lots of support and encouragement during this transition period.** If your dog goes to a former button location and whines, paws at it, or looks down to it, they are likely trying to communicate that word to you. Bring them over to the button mat and model the word for them a few times.

6 **Respond to all forms of communication.** Your dog may rely on other forms of communication more while figuring out their new setup. Make sure to acknowledge these forms of communication, then model the corresponding word so they can see where it is.

7 **Give it time.** Expect that this will be a process, not an instant solution. If after a few solid weeks of modeling words your dog hasn't made any progress with the new locations, you can consider moving the buttons back to their original locations.

Activities

1. Button Location Checklist

Now that you have a location in mind, ask yourself the following questions to make sure your buttons are set up for success. When you can say yes to all these statements, you are ready to start modeling your words and teaching your dog!

My dog's buttons . . .

Are centrally located in my home	
Are somewhere we naturally spend time with our dog	
Are audible from most rooms	
Have space on all sides for my dog to walk around / approach	
Have room next to or below to add more buttons in the future	

2. Label Your Buttons

When you've decided on locations for each of your buttons, it's time to label them! While your dog is not reading the words, labels will help make sure your buttons always get returned back to their designated spot in the right order. Labels will also help you know which button is which in your early days of modeling and will allow any visitors to use your dog's buttons with ease, too.

The Hunger for Words Talking Pet Button Mat comes with labels you can place under each button. Many of our button sets come with sticker icons you can place on top of each button, too.

Summary

Buttons should be placed in easily accessible places in order for you to model words and for your dog to use them. Dogs learn and memorize the locations of each button, which means after you choose where you want to keep your buttons, it's crucial to keep each button in the same spot.

CHAPTER 5
Modeling Language

Two common misconceptions about how dogs learn have taken over the training landscape, shaping how most of us view our pets:

Misconception 1: *Dogs need extrinsic rewards (like treats) to learn how to do something.*

Misconception 2: *Dogs need direct instructions and commands to acquire new skills.*

However, in the book *The Genius of Dogs* by Brian Hare and Vanessa Woods, the authors share stories and research studies of dogs learning new skills simply by watching someone else do them first. For example, puppies who were kept by their mother as she performed her drug-searching duties were compared to other puppies who hadn't seen these tasks completed. Results showed that the puppies who accompanied their mother on the job "were four times more likely to get the highest training scores than other puppies."

Dogs' capability to learn through imitation is a key reason why they can learn to use words meaningfully. Your dog will learn to use her buttons by watching and hearing *you* use her buttons throughout the day. This is called *modeling,* which is the most important strategy in teaching your dog to talk.

What Is Modeling Language and Why Does It Work?

The ability to imitate is a foundation of language development. Babies and young toddlers imitate a caregiver's gestures, sounds, and words before being able to generate them independently to communicate. *Modeling* here means using your dog's buttons in the right contexts. Every time you model a word for your dog, you are showing them an example of when and how they can say that word, too. Modeling words with your buttons allows your dog to progress through important stages of language development, just as humans do.

When you first introduce buttons to your dog, the primary focus should be on *your* modeling words, not on your dog's using the buttons. This is called *modeling without expectation*. Modeling without expectation provides your dog with the necessary exposure to the buttons in order to learn what they are and what they're for. Just like humans, dogs have to understand what words mean before being able to use them functionally and intentionally. We wouldn't expect a baby to immediately start talking after hearing words for the first time, so we shouldn't expect our dogs to immediately use words intentionally right when we introduce them. By modeling words in their appropriate contexts, you are teaching your dog the meaning of each button. Your patience will pay off!

After you've been modeling words consistently for a couple of weeks and your dog starts showing more awareness of the buttons, you can incorporate a few strategies to help your dog initiate use. But don't worry about this now. We'll cover it all in the next chapter!

What Does Modeling Look Like?

Modeling works best when it's incorporated throughout the naturally occurring routines of your days rather than during stand-alone training sessions. Modeling a word and giving your dog a chance to respond takes only about a minute to do. Instead of setting a large chunk of time each day to model words, aim to add small pockets of time built into your routines to talk about what's happening.

The two most important times to model words are as follows:

1. When You Are Saying a Word to Your Dog

As you narrate your dog's actions or what's happening in the environment around them, use her buttons, too. As a rule of thumb, if you're verbally saying a word that your dog has a button for, use her button as well. Here are a couple of examples:

- When you're feeding your dog, verbally say, "It's time to eat!" (Press *eat* button.) "Eat now." (Press *eat* button.) "Eat now." (Press *eat* button.) Feed your dog. While they're eating, say, "[Dog's name] eat!" (Press *eat* button.) When they're finished, you can wrap it up by saying, "All done eat." (Press *eat* button.)
- When you're getting ready to leave, say, "Bye!" (Press *bye* button.) *Bye, love you!* (Press *bye* and *love you* buttons.) "Bye now!" (Press *bye* button.) Finish getting ready to leave, then go.

In both examples, your dog is hearing and seeing the target word in use during appropriate contexts between six and ten times. Each of these interactions takes less than one minute. Short bursts of modeling words multiple times a day is much more effective than conducting longer training sessions a few times each week. The key takeaway here is that the frequency of modeling is more important than the duration of modeling.

2. When You Observe Your Dog Communicating the Meaning of a Word with Their Gestures, Body Language, or Vocalizations

Since the end goal is for your dog to use buttons to communicate independently, another excellent time to model words is when you observe your dog communicating a concept they have a button for. Remember, gestures pave the way for words. We want to build from your dog's current communication patterns and strengths. Take a look at Activity 1 on page 55 to figure out what you can model in different situations throughout your day.

How to Make Your Modeling Even *More* Effective

Have you ever observed a mother talking to her baby or toddler in a singsongy voice that's slower and higher pitched? This way of speaking, called *parentese,* draws a baby's attention to the speaker and helps them focus on words. Research shows that parentese occurs in cultures and languages around the world, and leads to increased language development outcomes for the baby.

Changing our tone of voice, our rate of speech, and the surrounding environment can all help our dogs pay closer attention to us and the words we're saying to them, too. When you're modeling words verbally and with your dog's buttons, try these simple tweaks to draw your dog's attention to you:

1   Slow down your rate of speech and exaggerate each syllable of multi-syllabic words.
2   Repeat your target word (the word you're pushing with your dog's button) several times in a row.
3   Soften your voice and raise your pitch, as if you were talking to a baby or young toddler.
4   Limit distractions in the surrounding area. Turn off the TV, any music, or other noises to keep your dog's focus and attention on you and the words you're saying.

Strategies to Avoid and Why

Commanding Your Dog to Push a Button or to Say a Word

Many people introduce buttons by training the "paw" or "touch" command first, then using this command to tell their dog to paw or touch the buttons. This is more like training your dog to do a trick than like teaching your dog how to communicate with a word. If you tell your dog what to do or what to say in the beginning, they are learning that the buttons are a tool you command them to use. When you use this as a foundation, it's difficult for your dog to unlearn this pattern and use the buttons completely independently in the future.

Enticing Your Dog to Be Near the Buttons with the Use of Treats

Another strategy I've seen people implement is holding treats above or near the button to entice their dog to come near it. Introducing treats in the mix can confuse the meaning of the button for your dog. Your dog may learn that the buttons lead to treats, not to their specific word meaning outcomes. This tactic is more similar to bribing your dog to interact with the buttons rather than teaching the meaning and power of the word.

Holding Your Dog's Paw to Push the Button

Communication is always a choice and should never be forced. We can't physically pull words out of someone's mouth who communicates with verbal speech, and learners who use communication devices deserve the same respect for their voice. Additionally, pushing your dog's paw down on the button can cause a negative association with the buttons, which we want to avoid.

Activities

1. Your Dog's Communication Patterns: Expanded

Below is a copy of the chart you completed in chapter 2, "Finding Your Dog's Current Communication Patterns." There is one more column added for you to write down words you can say and model during these activities. See my examples below, then complete your chart.

Example:

PROMPT	RESPONSE	DOMINANT FORM(S) OF COMMUNICATION	WHAT I CAN SAY AND DO
I know my dog needs to go outside when . . .	They stand near the door and whine	Positioning Whining	Label what I see. "You want outside!" (Press *outside* button.) "[Dog's name] wants outside." (Press *outside* button.) "Let's go outside!" (Press *outside* button.) Then open the door to go outside.
I know my dog wants to play when . . .	They bring me a toy	Joint attention	"Oh. you want to play!" (Press *play* button.) "Play, play, play." (Press *play* button.) "Let's play!" (Press *play* button.) Then play with your dog.
I feel most confused about what my dog is trying to tell me when . . .	They whine at me, but don't need to go out and have already been fed	Whining	Label what I see. "Stella wants something." Ask a question: "What does Stella want?" Pick a button to model and provide the action. Even if it wasn't what my dog was trying to tell me, she'll see me trying to understand and giving an example of how her buttons work.

In the examples above, your dog would have heard the word that corresponded to their communication between six and eight times. By pairing a word to your dog's gestures and vocalizations, you are teaching them the meaning of the word and showing them how they can say it, too. When you aren't sure what your dog is trying to communicate, you can pick a button to model and follow through with the corresponding action. You are still modeling the meaning of a button and the concept that buttons are for the purpose of communication.

Your turn!

PROMPT	RESPONSE	DOMINANT FORM(S) OF COMMUNICATION	WHAT I CAN SAY AND DO
I know my dog needs to go outside when . . .			
My dog shows me they're ready to eat by . . .			
I know my dog wants to go for a walk when . . .			
If my dog needs help with something, they usually . . .			
My dog wants my attention most when . . .			
I know my dog wants to play when . . .			
I can tell my dog is upset when . . .			
I can tell my dog is happy when . . .			
My dog shows they want affection when . . .			
I feel most confused about what my dog is trying to tell me when . . .			

2. Set Modeling Goals for Yourself

Creating achievable goals for yourself can help make modeling words a habit. Modeling is a skill you'll use throughout your button communication journey, so it's wise to become familiar and comfortable with it from the start. Planning ahead with times of days / activities that work for you can help you be successful with modeling right away. Use the information you completed in the chart above to help you think about when you can model words.

Beginner goal: I will use my dog's buttons before / during three different activities throughout the day.

Examples:

1   Before taking them outside in the morning (*outside*)
2   Before you feed them in the morning (*eat*)
3   In the afternoon when they try to get you to stop working and play with them (*play*)

Choose your activities and list them here:

1   _____
2   _____
3   _____

Once the beginner goal has become easy and part of your routine, move to the intermediate goal.

Intermediate goal: I will model each of my dog's buttons at least twice per day.

Summary

Dogs have the cognitive capabilities to learn information and skills similarly to how humans do. The most important strategy for teaching language is called *modeling*, which means using your dog's buttons in the right contexts. Your dog will learn how to use words by watching you use them in meaningful ways. Focus on building modeling into your daily routines. You will continue to model new and old words for your dog throughout their entire button communication journey.

CHAPTER 6

Supporting Your Unique Learner

Dogs have different personalities and learning styles, just as humans do. Part of the fun in teaching is learning more about your student, appreciating their strengths, and watching them grow. A dog's learning style, age, and personality can all impact how they respond to buttons. The advice in this section will help you determine your dog's learning style, cater your teaching to them, and troubleshoot obstacles you may come across. You'll also find tips for teaching in a multi-pet home or supporting a dog with special needs.

Discover Your Dog's Learning Style

After you've set your buttons up and begun modeling, you should be able to tell which type of learner your dog is pretty quickly. Generally, there are two types of button learners: *exploratory* and *observant*. Understanding your dog's learning style can help you immensely in the early stages of introducing buttons. Exploratory learners tend to learn primarily from exploring their buttons and seeing how their communication partner responds. Observant learners tend to learn mostly through watching their humans use the buttons for a while. Their interest in using the buttons themselves increases over time after observing patterns. Exploratory learners and observant learners require slightly different approaches. Take a look at the characteristics below to familiarize yourself with the two different learning styles.

Exploratory Learner Characteristics

- Immediate interest and curiosity in the buttons, even before knowing what they're for.
- Looks like: dog pawing at buttons when you set them on the ground, walking all around buttons and attempting to interact with them, pushing buttons repeatedly, pushing multiple buttons in a row, playing with buttons.

Observant Learner Characteristics

- No strong, obvious signs of interest right away. They might not even appear to be paying attention as you model words or try to show your dog what the buttons do.
- Looks like: dog seemingly ignoring the buttons, dog watching you use the buttons without attempting to engage with them.

Activities

1. How to Respond to Exploratory Learners

With exploratory learners, the interest is immediately there, but you have to teach your dog what the buttons are actually for. The number one goal is shaping this natural curiosity into intentional communication.

Here's what you can do:

- Encourage your dog's exploration by saying "yes" or "good girl" when you see this level of interaction and engagement
- Respond with the meaning of the word they're exploring. If your dog is pushing the *outside* button repeatedly (or even just once) say, "Okay, yes, let's go outside!" and take them out.
- If your dog is babbling (pushing lots of different buttons in a row), let them. Wait until they're done, then model one of the words they said and provide the appropriate response.
- Know that these first words may not be intentional yet, but it's an important step in their learning process to have opportunities to engage with the buttons and see how you respond to them.

2. How to Engage Observant Learners

Observant learners take more time to interact with their buttons, but often end up using them intentionally from the start when they do. After you've spent a solid couple of weeks modeling words, this is what you can do to help your learner engage with their buttons:

- Give your dog more pause time. After modeling a word, pause for a solid thirty seconds to give your dog the opportunity to explore their buttons. After pausing, you can say something like "You can try" while pointing to the buttons. Wait again. After another thirty seconds, if they haven't interacted with their buttons at all, model the word once more and carry on with your activity.
- Praise your dog ("Yes, good girl!") when you catch them watching you model a word, looking at their buttons, standing near them at all, or attempting to interact with them.
- Follow their lead. Don't try forcing your dog to come by the buttons or to try saying a word. This can cause a negative association with the buttons or have buttons viewed as work instead of a tool for communicating throughout their day.
- Spend time sitting near the buttons without modeling words. Pet your dog near the buttons, play near them. The more time you spend around them, the more likely they'll be to accidentally hit a button or to explore intentionally. When they do say a word (accidentally or not), this gives you the great opportunity to respond with the meaning of the word.

Age-Specific Advice

While the general way to teach puppies and older dogs to use buttons is the same, there are a couple of tweaks you can make to help you with whichever stage of life your learner is in.

Teaching Puppies

Puppies tend to have shorter attention spans than older dogs, so you'll want to focus on providing as many repetitions as possible when you do have their attention. Aim to repeat a word three to five times while your puppy is focused on an activity. These extra repetitions will help your puppy solidify the meanings of words, too. Just as with humans, dogs have to understand words before they're able to say words intentionally. Puppies may be naturally curious and ready to explore their buttons, but they still need time to learn the meanings of words before you can expect them to use their buttons independently.

Teaching Adult Dogs

Adult dogs tend to have longer attention spans than puppies. Since your older dog likely already understands the meanings of the words you're teaching, focus more on giving your dog extra wait / processing time rather than bombarding them with repetitions of words. Still repeat a word a couple of times, but if your dog hasn't moved on to something else, stay quiet and give your dog a chance to respond or explore their buttons. Older dogs are completely capable of learning new skills. Stay patient and consistent to give them the opportunity to learn!

Dogs with Special Needs

Dogs with special needs are capable of learning to talk with buttons, too! During the last few years, I have found it incredible to work with and see dogs who are deaf, blind, and even deafblind using buttons to communicate. With some tweaks to teaching styles and added supports along the way, your dog can still learn to use words. Here's what you can do to help your dog with different impairments.

Hearing Impairments

Dogs who are deaf or hearing impaired can watch you model words and see what happens right after you press a button, but they can't hear what the button says when pressed. If your dog was born deaf and you use any sort of hand signals or gestures to communicate to your pup, you can use these same hand signals as you're modeling your buttons. This is the equivalent of saying a word verbally while pressing the button for it. Even though your dog won't be able to hear the word the button says, still program it, because this is how *you* will hear what your dog is saying if you aren't right there. Responding to your dog's button presses is especially important when you're teaching a dog with a hearing impairment. When your dog engages with the buttons at all, respond with the action they said. Your dog will draw connections between the button they pressed and what happened in their environment even though they aren't receiving the auditory input.

If you do not use hand signals with your dog, or your dog is losing their hearing with age, you can start implementing more gestures in your communication now. As you talk to your dog, pair your words with informal gestures. As you press the *outside* button and say "outside," you can point to the door and walk to it. As you say "play" verbally and with your dog's button, you can point to or touch your dog's toy basket. The more types of input and cues your dog is receiving, the better for learning.

Visual Impairments

Dogs who are blind or visually impaired can hear what each button says when pressed, but can't watch you model words. Dogs who are visually impaired can still form motor plans for different locations like dogs who can see do. Dogs who are blind memorize where physical objects are in their environments so they can navigate around with ease. Keeping buttons in the same order and overall location is especially important for dogs with visual impairments. When they learn where a button is, they will return to that same space expecting it to be there again. When setting up buttons for a visually impaired dog, I recommend adding extra space between buttons to make each location more distinct. If you're using a button mat, you can fill every other spot.

Working with visually impaired dogs is the only situation in which I suggest giving a verbal command to "paw" or "touch" a button in the beginning stages of learning. Since your dog isn't able to watch what you're doing, a verbal cue can help your dog become aware of the buttons and understand what to do. You can bring your dog near her buttons, give her your "paw" or "touch" command, and have her press down on a button. Whichever one she presses, repeat the word back to her that she said verbally and with the button. Then respond immediately with the action of the word.

One difference you may notice when working with your visually impaired dog is the use of *auditory scanning* in their communication. Auditory scanning means pressing each button to hear what it says before making a selection. Dogs may press multiple times on the button they're selecting, or they may stop pressing other buttons after they found the intended button. If you notice your dog pressing multiple buttons in a row, especially in the early stages of learning, she is likely listening for the one she's looking for. You can respond to the last button she selects and provide that action.

You can also consider adding different textures to the button tops. This is recommended for deafblind dogs, but visually impaired dogs may benefit from this as well. Taping different textures to the button tops would allow your dog to feel the difference between buttons on their paws before even pressing the button. See below for texture ideas.

Deafblind Dogs

Dogs who are deafblind aren't able to watch you model words or hear what the button says, but they can feel different textures, form motor plans for different button locations, and understand what happens in their environment around them after pressing a button. If your dog is deafblind, you likely have touch or tap signals that you give your dog in order to communicate to them (for example, tapping a certain location or number of times on their body to indicate different concepts). If you don't use tap or touch signals, I highly recommend starting to implement these as soon as possible.

Before starting to work with your dog, you'll want to put different textures on each button top. One button can remain in its original form without an added texture on top. Your dog will draw associations between the different textures and what happens in their environment after pressing them. Below are a few different texture ideas, but feel free to get creative:

Suggestions for Textures to Tape on Button Tops
- Velcro (both the fuzzy and scratchy sides)
- Fabric from a plush toy
- Fake grass turf
- Paper

If your deafblind dog has a solid understanding of a "come" signal, you can use this to bring your dog over to the buttons. Then you can signal for your dog to paw or touch where the buttons are. Your dog may choose to use their nose or paw; either one is perfectly fine. Working with a deafblind dog is the only instance in which I recommend using some physical cues to help their paw to the button if needed. Don't grab their paw and push the button for them, but if your dog is close to the button, you can help guide their paw in the direction of it and gently apply enough pressure.

If using a "come" and "touch" signal does not work to bring your dog over to the buttons, you can try holding a treat above the button and having your dog paw to get the treat out of your closed fist. This is the only time I suggest using a treat to help your dog learn to push a button. As your dog is pawing, you'll want to have them "accidentally" hit the button. Whenever your dog does hit the button, provide the appropriate action of whichever button she pressed.

Teaching sessions with your deafblind dog, especially in the beginning, will be more structured. As your dog learns that the buttons exist and where to find them, you may notice more natural exploration and babbling.

Teaching in a Multi-Pet Home

Teaching multiple animals to talk is an exciting venture! You'll likely see the differences in your pets come out through their learning styles, communication styles, and topic choices. While the process of teaching dogs to talk is the same whether you're teaching one or two dogs, there are a few factors to keep in mind to set you and your pets up for success.

1. Dogs Learn from Each Other and from You

As we learned in the last chapter, dogs can learn just by watching another dog perform a skill or task. This means that if one of your dogs starts to use buttons, the other will likely be learning from your modeling and from your dog. In my experiences working with multi-pet homes, typically one dog takes the lead on using buttons first. If you have one dog who is more interested in the buttons than the other, you can follow their lead and spend more time modeling directly for them.

2. Each Pet Will Likely Have Different Communication Styles

Buttons magnify differences in personalities. Dogs' word choices are reflections of their minds. Try to celebrate what makes each pet unique rather than attempting to get each to use buttons in the same ways as the other. A favorite word or phrase for one pet may be one rarely used by your other pet.

3. Use Names to Your Advantage

With more people or animals in the home, there is naturally more you can narrate about what's happening. Program your pets' names into the buttons earlier on in your teaching and talk about what each one of them is doing. One dog may talk about what the other is doing, just as your dogs may narrate what you're doing, too.

What to Do If . . .

Your Dog Is Scared of the Buttons

Some dogs become nervous with objects that make new sounds. If your dog displays signs of fear such as running away from the buttons or aggressively barking at them, you'll want to go very slowly with your teaching. In this case, the top priority is not for your dog to use buttons right away. It's to help your dog feel comfortable and safe around them. Follow this procedure if your dog shows signs of fear:

1   Stop modeling words. Start by keeping buttons out in your home for your dog to get used to visually.

2   After a few days to a week of having buttons out in your home, start intentionally spending time around the buttons with your dog. You can sit near the buttons and rub your dog's belly or give them scratches, play near the buttons, and do other types of training they enjoy near the buttons.

3   Praise your dog whenever they are comfortably near the buttons. If they're tolerating play near the buttons or walking close to them, say "Yes!" and give them lots of positive attention.

4   After a few days to a week, start modeling words again when your dog is not immediately nearby the buttons. When they're across the room or in an adjacent room, use your dog's buttons to talk about what you're about to do or what is happening. Don't put any pressure on your dog to come watch you or to interact with the buttons.

5   When your dog is tolerating you modeling words when they're farther away, start modeling words when your dog is closer to the buttons. Observe to see how your dog responds. If they become fearful again, go back to modeling words from a distance.

6 Once your dog tolerates you modeling words when they're nearby, continue teaching as usual.

Your Dog Is Overly Playful with the Buttons

It's normal for your dog to paw at the buttons and push around on different words to hear what they say. Exploration and natural curiosity form the basis of how they'll learn! But if your dog picks up the buttons and carries them around, paws or noses them around the floor like they're toys, or starts chewing on them, follow these steps:

1 Avoid saying no or scolding your dog. We want to keep your dog's association with their buttons as positive as possible to encourage future interactions and use. Instead of saying no, go to step 2.

2 Redirect! If your dog is trying to play with the buttons, redirect their attention to something that they *can* play with. Grab a toy and swap it out. This is the perfect opportunity to model the word *play*. Praise your dog when they start playing with the toy. If your dog keeps going for the buttons instead, take them off the floor temporarily. Return them when your dog is finished playing with their toy.

3 If your dog picks up buttons and brings them around the house, try securing them even more to your surface. Invest in a button mat if you don't already have one. If you already have one, try Velcroing the buttons within the mat to keep it extra locked in.

4 If your dog starts chewing on the buttons, swap it out with something they can safely chew instead. Praise your dog when they chew on the object you swapped instead. Do not leave your dog unattended with their buttons until they learn not to chew on them.

5 Continue modeling words during appropriate contexts to show your dog how and when to use their words. The more your dog sees what the buttons are for, the more they'll learn how to use them appropriately.

Your Dog Isn't Paying Attention When You Model Words

This is completely normal in the beginning. Keep modeling, even if it doesn't look like your dog is paying attention to you or watching what you're doing. At the very least, they're hearing your words and hearing what the button says.

Don't try forcing your dog to come over and watch you or look at you while you're pressing the buttons. Interest and curiosity often build naturally over time, and you don't want to create a negative association with them. In the next chapter, you'll learn more strategies to draw your dog's attention to the buttons at the right times. For now, don't force it.

Summary

While the same core strategies can guide most of your teaching, there are specific modifications you can make for different learning styles, puppies, older dogs, multi-pet homes, and dogs with special needs. Keep these modifications in mind as you continue adding words and teaching new concepts.

CHAPTER 7

Identifying Signs of Progress and First Words

When I first introduced buttons to Stella, I had no idea what was possible. For a full two to three weeks, Stella didn't acknowledge her buttons at all. I couldn't even tell if she knew they were there or not. But, a few weeks into modeling words, I noticed slight changes in her behavior around the buttons, which encouraged me to continue on.

Typically, Stella looked around everywhere except for the button when I modeled words. She was only a few months old and had a fleeting attention span. Everything in her environment was still new to her.

One day while I was grabbing a snack from the fridge, I turned around to see Stella standing near the back door where her *outside* button was set up. I hadn't modeled a word or said anything, but Stella was staring directly down at her button. This was the first time I had seen Stella look at her button for more than a second in passing. The best part was that it was completely unprompted. She independently walked to that area and stared down at her button with undivided attention.

I quickly closed the fridge door and joined her. "Yes, good girl, Stella!" I said. From my experience working with kids, I knew that providing encouragement, even during these small milestones, often inspires learners to keep exploring their words in the future.

Stella wagged her tail and licked my face.

"Outside," I said verbally and with her button. "Come outside!" This time Stella watched me closely as I pushed the button and followed me right out to the backyard.

To the outside observer, my puppy's looking at her button once in three weeks would probably not be an indication that she was learning or on the cusp of a breakthrough. But sometimes the slightest changes in behavior are actually an indication of increased awareness, readiness to learn, and understanding of the button's power. Just one week after Stella started showing these signs of progress, she said her first word, *outside,* when she needed to go to the bathroom.

When you know what to look for, you'll be able to detect these subtle signs of progress, too. Celebrating these milestones will give you the hope you need to keep teaching and your dog the encouragement and support they need to keep learning a new skill.

Typical Timelines

"How long does it take for dogs to learn?" is one of the most frequently asked questions I receive. I'm sure it won't surprise you to hear the answer is that every dog is different. A dog's age, environment, and personality all contribute to how they learn, along with their human's teaching style and consistency. Just as with humans, there is a wide range of normal when it comes to acquiring language. Even though you can't know exactly how long it will take your dog to learn, there are patterns you can watch for and signs that you and your dog are on the right track.

When we surveyed over 1,000 pet parents who have implemented buttons with their dogs, 65 percent of respondents shared that their dog began using their first word less than one month after introducing buttons. The second highest response was less than two months after introducing buttons.

As a result of my experience with teaching Stella and working one-on-one with hundreds of humans teaching their own companion animals to talk, I can confidently say that learning to use first words takes the longest amount of time. Typically, once learners understand the concept of the buttons and have success using a couple of different words, they catch on to other vocabulary much faster. This time period of introducing buttons before seeing your dog use them is the hardest part of the journey for the teacher. You're providing so much input and waiting to see the fruits of your labor.

If you're in this stage currently, please know that it does get easier. Right now your dog is learning what words mean, what happens when you press the buttons, and how they can use the buttons themselves. In the future, once they have the skill of pushing buttons with an intention in mind and know that the buttons serve a communicative purpose, they'll need to learn only the meaning of the new words you introduce, a process that will be much quicker. All the work you're doing now is setting your dog up for success and providing a really solid foundation for them to use words independently in the future.

Before First Words

Before your dog starts using buttons intentionally and independently to communicate, you'll likely see a variety of skills emerge first. This is consistent with human language development. Babies and toddlers don't just start talking overnight. They build up to saying words. First they babble, use gestures such as pointing or clapping, imitate your words, then say words completely on their own in the right contexts. It's a pattern similar to that of dogs getting to the point of using buttons. Below are some of the subtle behaviors you may see during your teaching journey, along with their significance and how you can respond most effectively. All these subtle changes in your dog's behavior around the buttons are indicative of great progress. Get excited when you see any of these—your dog is learning!

SKILL	WHAT IT LOOKS LIKE	SIGNIFICANCE	WHAT YOU SHOULD DO
Joint attention	• Your dog watching you model words • Your dog looking at the button and looking to you	Shared attention is a major language milestone. When you and your dog are both focused on the same object (the buttons), the most learning happens. Your dog is directing your attention to the button via their eye gaze.	Encourage your dog. Say, "Yes!" and show that you're excited to see them looking at the buttons. Model the word for them, then pause. Give your dog a chance to try. After your pause, model one more time and carry on.

SKILL	WHAT IT LOOKS LIKE	SIGNIFICANCE	WHAT YOU SHOULD DO
Vocalizing near buttons	• Your dog barking or whining at the buttons • Your dog barking or whining at you while near their buttons	Your dog has learned that the buttons are meaningful. They are trying to get your attention to push the buttons and make something happen.	Acknowledge your dog's communication and provide encouragement. Say,"I hear you. What do you want?" Pause and give them a chance to respond. Point to the buttons. If there's no response, try modeling a word you think they might be trying to communicate. Wait to see how they respond, and carry on with the activity if they seem interested.
Gesturing near buttons	• Your dog swatting near the buttons and missing • Your dog gently touching the buttons • Your dog circling around the buttons	Your dog is attempting to interact with the buttons, but still needs a little help from you.	Acknowledge your dog's communication and help them. If they tried hitting a specific button, say, "Yes, good girl!" and model it for them. Carry on with the activity. Don't try forcing them to get it 100 percent right before responding.
Babbling	• Your dog pushing multiple buttons in a row when they want something • Your dog pushing any button (normally whichever is closest) to get your attention	Your dog is demonstrating communicative intent. When they want or need something, they know to go to their buttons, but haven't distinguished the different meanings of individual buttons as yet.	Respond to what your dog says as if it were intentional. This is how they will learn the power and meaning of each word. After you respond, if that's not what they wanted, give them time to try again or model the word you think they might have meant.

Responding to Your Dog as They're Learning

By reviewing the chart above, you can see a few main common themes in your responses: *acknowledging your dog, pausing,* and *providing encouragement.* The more patience and support you give your dog as they're learning, the more you'll empower them to develop a new skill and to be able to share all that's on their mind with you.

When in doubt, acknowledge your dog's attempts to use the buttons or other forms of communication. By acknowledging what you're seeing, you're establishing a positive relationship based on mutual communication. Your dog is learning that they can count on you to respond to their communication, which will encourage them to keep communicating with you! You can acknowledge your dog with simple statements like: "Yes, I hear you"; "Yes, good girl"; and "Yes, you're trying."

After you've acknowledged what you observe, take time to pause. Stay quiet and still. Your dog needs time to process what's happening in the environment, what they want to say, and how to try saying it. Aim to stay quiet for a solid thirty to sixty seconds. If your dog is about to walk away, you can cut the pause time short and model a word relevant to what's happening or what you're about to do. Providing a long pause is the simplest thing you can do, but it's often the hardest for people to execute in the moment. For the most part, we're all used to conversing with adults, whose language skills are completely developed. We can generate our ideas quickly and say them immediately. But your dog needs time to think. This extended pause will also serve as a cue to your dog that it's her turn to talk. You are making space in the interaction for her to share what she wants to share.

Finally, remember to provide encouragement along the way. Show your dog that you're proud of them for trying. You can say "Yes!" or "Good girl," clap, or pet them. Just make sure to avoid giving your dog a treat for saying a word or for trying to interact with their buttons—this will confuse the meaning of the button for them.

Cues

When you see your dog demonstrating any of the skills in the above chart, you can start giving them more cues during your interactions around the buttons, too. Cues are helpful reminders for your dog as they're learning. Since the end goal is for your dog to use their buttons independently, it's best to give cues that offer the least amount of support first. Work your way up to cues that provide the most support. Giving too much support when it's not needed can inhibit your dog from trying to use the buttons on their own. By starting with cues that offer the least amount of support, you can ensure that you won't be over-cueing.

Cues Listed in Order of Support Provided (Least to Most)

1. Increased pause time

By staying silent for thirty to sixty seconds, you are cueing your dog that it's their turn to talk. Start with a pause, then move down the list of cues if the pause alone doesn't work.

2. Sitting or standing near the buttons

Your sitting or standing near the buttons while you're staying quiet can serve as a gentle reminder, too. Your being near the buttons can encourage your dog to come over and try saying a word.

3. Pointing generally to the buttons

Pointing to the general direction of the buttons (not to a specific button) can draw your dog's attention to their words and encourage them to try using one.

4. Open-ended verbal prompt

Asking a general question such as "What do you want?" or saying something like "You can tell me" is another way to elicit a response. Remember to pause after your statement to give your dog a chance to respond.

5. Tapping next to a button or pointing directly to a button

If you're targeting a certain word, you can point right above it or tap the ground directly next to the button in order to draw your dog's attention there.

6. Provide a direct model

Finally, model a word you think your dog might be trying to communicate and carry on with the activity it represents. Don't worry about getting it wrong. Even if you choose a word your dog wasn't trying to say, you're still providing an example of how the word you modeled can be used.

Knowing What's Intentional

When your dog starts using their buttons, you might be wondering *"Did they really mean that? Was it a coincidence?"* Because it's not always 100 percent clear if a word was intentional or exploratory, especially in the beginning, it's best to respond as if it was intentional. In the worst-case scenario, your dog was exploring a button or accidentally said something, and you showed what it meant by responding to them. If you assume a word was not intentional, the worst-case scenario is that your dog did truly mean it and then their communication was ignored. We would much rather have the first scenario! It's impossible to know what another being is capable of or what is in their mind. Your dog may surprise you with what they're thinking about! Stay open to the possibilities that your dog may come up with unexpected words or phrases.

With that being said, there are characteristics that you can look for to determine if your dog is babbling or using words intentionally. As a speech therapist, I use these criteria when working with kids learning to use communication devices:

Context / Environment

What's going on in the environment around your dog currently? Does the word they said make sense for what they're doing, what you're doing, or what would normally be happening at this time of day?

Nonverbal Communication

What other forms of communication are your dog exhibiting right now? Do they align with the word they just said?

Patterns

Is this the first time they've said a word in this context, or is it becoming a pattern? Repetition typically means intention.

Level of Support Provided

How much cueing did you provide, if any? The fewer the cues given, the more we know the words are coming from the learner, not from what the learner thinks you want them to say.

Language Level

Does what your dog said make sense for their overall language level and communication trends? While we never want to limit anyone's potential or capabilities, it's important to look at what was said through a lens of practicality. For example, if your dog has only ever said single words at a time and is just learning to use their buttons, a four- or five-word combination may have been them searching for the word they wanted to say rather than a true independent phrase.

Your Dog's Response to Your Response

When you respond to their word(s), do they seem content? Or do they try saying something else? If they try using other forms of communication or a different word, this could mean either the interpretation was wrong or your dog meant to say something else.

Frequently Asked Questions About First Words

What should I do if I can't say yes to what my dog asks for?

Inevitably, there will be times when you can't say yes and that is completely fine! You can still respond to your dog and acknowledge what they said without saying yes. For example, if your dog says *park* in the middle of the day while you're working, you can respond by saying something like "Park? I heard you say park. We'll go to the park later. Park later." Your repeating the word back to your dog lets them know that you heard what they said even if you can't go right now.

In the very beginning (your dog's first few interactions with the buttons), try your best to provide the activity they requested so they know that the buttons have power. Even if you can't give the full scope of the activity, try a reduced version. For example, if your dog says *walk* at a time when you can't take them out for a full walk, could you put their leash on and walk them to the end of your driveway or down the street quickly?

As your dog keeps learning, it's okay to say "no," "all done," or "later." Think about a toddler asking their parent for cookies all day. The parent can respond to what they're saying without saying yes.

My dog has used their buttons, but they don't use them every single time they need something. What should I do?

Even after your dog starts using their buttons, it will take time before they start using them during most of their interactions with you. Keep providing support (modeling, pause time, other cues). When your dog starts initiating use more and responding quicker, begin to lessen the cues you're giving them. This will help your dog become more automatic with their buttons. In Part Two of this guidebook, you'll find more information on promoting independence and increasing communication frequency.

Remember, your dog's buttons are another tool in their communication toolbox to express themselves to you. The buttons will not completely replace your dog's other forms of communication.

My dog uses one button to mean everything. What should I do?

Pet parents often find themselves in this situation if they respond to what their dog said with what they think their dog meant instead of what was actually said. In this case, their dog has seen a variety of responses come from a single word, which is why they keep using that word.

Respond to the word they say only with its meaning. Increase your modeling of other buttons and provide the activity to show what they mean.

Another reason this could be happening is because your dog doesn't have enough vocabulary. If they have only a couple of words, they might use these words to mean everything. Try adding a few more buttons if this is the case.

Activities

1. Video Reflection

In graduate school, we were required to film a certain number of speech therapy sessions each month, watch the videos of them, and write a reflection. Even though I sometimes felt uncomfortable watching myself, nothing was more powerful in helping me become a better teacher. Often what we think we're doing and what we're actually doing are very different. To this day, I learn the most about both my teaching skills and Stella's communication through watching videos of our interactions. You can do this, too!

Take a video of yourself modeling words for your dog and answer these questions as you watch it back:

How many times did you talk during this interaction?

_____

How many times did you pause to give your dog a chance to talk or respond?

_____

How long did you pause for? (Count the seconds!)

_____

What cues (modeling, pause time, gestures, verbal prompts) did you give your dog?

_____

Did your dog respond to one type of cue more than others?

_____

What could you improve on next time?

_____

2. Recordkeeping

Your dog's first word is a special milestone! Record the details here to look back at for years to come.

First Word:

_____

Date:

_____

Amount of time after introducing buttons (e.g., one week, one month, etc.):

_____

Context:

_____

_____

_____

_____

Summary

Before your dog uses words intentionally, there will be signs of progress that they're learning. In these early stages, your dog can benefit from gentle cues to help them know what to do with the buttons. Offer the smallest number of cues that your dog needs in order to use their buttons. This will lead to your dog using their buttons independently rather than only when you tell or ask them to.

CHAPTER 8

Promoting Independence

Throughout your dog's button communication journey, different levels of assistance will be required at different times. Knowing how much support you're giving your dog can help you make decisions about when to add more words and what to target next. Your goal shouldn't always be to add more words. Goals can also be to help your dog become more independent with their current vocabulary or to use words in different contexts. We'll talk about the former in this chapter and the latter later on in chapter 9. *The end goal is for your dog to be able to use a majority of their words independently or with minimal support.* When your dog reaches this stage, you can be confident that no matter who they're with or what they're doing, they will always have a way to express their thoughts, wants, and needs.

Levels of Support

There are four main levels of support you can offer while teaching your dog to talk: maximum, moderate, minimum, and no support. The types of cues you're giving your dog determine the level of support you're providing. A good way to think about this is imagining a child learning to walk. The child doesn't start walking independently immediately. First they might grip furniture with two hands and cruise (maximum support). Then they might cruise with one hand (moderate support). After that, you might see the child lightly hold a caregiver's hand (minimal support). Finally, the child will be taking steps independently (no support).

The chart below shows how these different levels of support look when cued by you and in practice with your dog.

LEVEL OF SUPPORT	CUES GIVEN BY YOU	WHAT IT LOOKS LIKE
Maximum	Direct model	Your dog using their buttons after you've modeled words for them
Moderate	• Open-ended verbal prompt • Tapping next to a button • Pointing to a specific button	Your dog using their buttons after you ask what they want or gesture to a specific button
Minimum	• Pointing generally to the buttons • Sitting or standing near buttons • Increased pause time	Your dog using their buttons after you give an extended wait time or position yourself near the buttons
No support (independently)	None	Your dog walking up to their buttons on their own, without any encouragement from you (You might even be doing something else while this happens.)

How to Promote More Independence

When your dog starts using their buttons, it's completely normal for them to continue needing cues. But with more practice and with support from you that wanes as they improve, they'll learn how to initiate button use completely on their own. Follow these three steps to help your dog become more independent with their buttons:

1. Determine how much support you're currently providing.

Take a look at the above chart and think about your interactions with your dog around their buttons. If you're not sure which cues you're currently giving, try recording yourself or looking back to Activity 1, "Video Reflection," in chapter 7 (page 80). It's important to note that your dog will likely be at different levels of independence for different words. They may be independent with a couple of words, yet need moderate support for less used vocabulary.

2. Set your goal.

Once you've established the level of support you're currently giving, set a goal for your dog to be able to use her words with the next lowest level of support. You can use the chart below to keep track of what words your dog is using, how much support you're currently giving, and what your goal is.

Example:

WORD	CURRENT LEVEL OF SUPPORT	GOAL LEVEL OF SUPPORT
Outside	Minimal	No support
Play	Minimal	No support
Eat	Moderate	Minimal
Water	Moderate	Minimal
Love You	Maximum	Moderate
Walk	Maximum	Moderate

WORD	CURRENT LEVEL OF SUPPORT	GOAL LEVEL OF SUPPORT

3. Adjust the types of cues you're giving.

Now that you know what level of support you're providing and what your goal is, it's time to adjust how you're interacting with your dog around their buttons.

The number one way to help your dog use their buttons more independently is to add more pause time within your interactions. Before giving any cues, start with an exaggerated wait time (at least thirty to sixty seconds, but it could be up to two or three minutes). This means when you see your dog using

another form of communication (whining or barking at you, standing near a desired object, pawing or gesturing), stay silent before doing anything else. If the exaggerated wait time alone doesn't work, start working your way through the cue list we discussed in chapter 7:

1   Increased pause time
2   Sitting or standing near buttons
3   Pointing generally to the buttons
4   Giving an open-ended verbal prompt
5   Tapping next to a button or pointing directly to a button
6   Providing a direct model

When you reach your targeted level, add more pause time again and observe how your dog responds. If they don't use a word after this second extended pause time, continue adding these wait times within your interactions and deliberately moving through the cueing hierarchy. Keep in mind that you may also see different results during different times of day. There may be times when your dog has more or less patience, more or less urgency, or more interest in their words. This is completely normal, so keep at it!

When Is a Word "Learned"?

In chapter 6 we discussed the differences between babbling and intentional word use. But what happens when you see your dog using a word intentionally? Does this mean it has been officially learned?

In speech therapy, we would often create goals for children to use a word independently a few times over the course of a certain number of sessions. When a child reached that goal, it meant that they had learned how to use the targeted word.

When you see your dog use a word three different times independently in appropriate contexts, you can count that word as being learned. Your dog may have mastered a word before the third time you see them use it, but waiting until you see this third use can ensure that you're modeling and providing support if they're still figuring out exactly what the word means and how to use it. If your dog uses words in the right context but only when prompted, these concepts haven't yet been mastered. Knowing when your dog has mastered a word can help you make the most of your teaching time. You can shift your focus to targeting other concepts or growing your dog's vocabulary.

Activities

What to Do If . . .

1. Your dog relies on you to push her buttons.

If your dog understands the buttons and waits for you to use them, they have learned that the buttons are a tool for you to let them know what's happening. This is not a bad thing! It likely means you have done a great job modeling words consistently for your dog. Now it's time to shift your approach to help them understand that they can use the buttons, too.

When you notice your dog demonstrating other forms of communication or are at the time of day when one of their routines would be starting, hold off on modeling a word. Instead, stand near their buttons to give them a very subtle cue and stay silent. Provide an extended wait period (at least thirty to sixty seconds). Start working your way down the cue list, waiting until the last step to provide a direct model.

2. Your dog has learned to say a button on command.

There's a big difference between a dog talking independently and a dog using their buttons when given a command, such as "say outside." If your dog only uses their buttons when you tell them exactly what to say, they have learned to follow a direction from you, not to use the buttons when they have something to say. If this has happened, you must immediately stop giving your dog the verbal command to say a word. Instead, replace this with more pause time and other subtle cues (items 2 to 4 on the hierarchy). This will help your dog learn to use the buttons on their own.

Summary

The end goal is for your dog to be able to use their buttons independently in the right contexts, but there are four levels of support you can offer your dog while teaching them: maximum, moderate, minimum, and no support. The level of support is determined by the types of cues you give your dog as you're interacting with their buttons. Being aware of how much support you're giving your dog is important in helping them become an independent communicator.

PART TWO

INTERMEDIATE LEARNERS

Signs Your Dog Is an Intermediate Learner

- Your dog uses between six and ten words.
- Your dog says multiple different words every day.
- Your dog uses their buttons all on their own.
- Your dog is starting to combine words.
- Your dog uses words for purposes other than requesting.

CHAPTER 9

Growing Vocabulary

Welcome to Part Two of *Your Dog Can Talk*! If you're here, you've successfully introduced words to your dog, seen your dog use multiple words on their own, and have a solid foundation in button communication. This is no small feat—congratulations! I hope you can take a moment to be proud of all the progress you've made and be proud of your dog for learning this new skill.

When I first started teaching Stella to talk, I set out only to give her a clear way to say words for a few different basic needs. After I saw what she was capable of learning and how she began using words in unique ways, the real fun began. I continued adding vocabulary to give Stella the ability to express concepts more specific than those she could communicate via gestures alone, and words that served purposes other than simply requesting. This stage is when it started to feel like Stella and I were really sharing a language. I'm thrilled to be helping you achieve this same feeling of understanding with your own canine companion.

When and How to Add More Words

Introducing new words is one of my favorite parts of teaching. New words offer so much potential to hear what's on our learner's mind, see what they're capable of, and understand them on an even deeper level. Aside from the communication benefits, adding vocabulary is also an excellent way to provide your dog with more mental stimulation. Dogs love new challenges and are naturally curious creatures, so introducing new buttons can give your pup something novel to explore, focus on, and engage with.

Five Indicators That Your Dog Is Ready for More Words

1. They use all or most of their beginner vocabulary.

The most obvious sign that your dog is ready for more words is when they have used all or most of their beginner vocabulary buttons intentionally. The only way for your dog to learn how to say new words is to have new words available to them. This means when you're actively teaching your pup, you should always have at least a couple of words that they're still learning.

2. They start to make word combinations.

If your dog has used most of their words intentionally and started combining words together that don't make sense, they're likely trying to communicate something that they don't have a button for. Take this as a sign to increase their vocab and introduce some new concepts! If they're making word combinations that *do* make sense, that is even more of a sign that they're ready for more words.

3. They seem frustrated around their buttons (whining, pawing around at several buttons when trying to get your attention).

This is another telltale indicator that your dog is trying to say something but doesn't have the word available. If you have an idea of what they might be trying to tell you based on what's happening and their other forms of communication, introduce a word for that concept and try modeling it.

4. They use some words consistently, but haven't taken to the other buttons they have available.

There's always an element of trial and error with button communication. We try our best to pick words that we think our dogs would want to say, but we don't always get it right. If your dog is using a subset of their buttons consistently but not showing interest in others, that could indicate that they simply don't want to use those words right now. Adding more vocabulary can help you trial different concepts to learn if this is the problem or if there's something else going on.

5. They're going through times of transition.

Maybe you're moving, welcoming a new baby, visiting a new park semi-regularly, or taking your dog to daycare a few times a week. New routines warrant new words!

Cadence for Adding Vocabulary

When you've decided it's time to increase your dog's vocabulary, remember the 2–4 rule:

It's best to introduce two to four new buttons at a time every two to four weeks.

This number of words allows you to try a variety of concepts without making a drastic change to your button setup and system each time. Allowing two to four weeks for each batch of new words gives your dog time to process and learn, while also keeping you in a good teaching flow. If your dog catches on quickly and you want to add more words sooner, or you have a busy period coming up and wait longer than a month to increase vocabulary, that's also okay. The 2–4 rule is a guidepost, but you and your dog can absolutely be successful within other timelines, too.

When selecting your batches of two to four words, try adding concepts that go together at the same time. Examples are words that fall in the same category (e.g., *park* and *beach* are both locations you visit outside your house) or words that have opposite meanings (e.g., *come* and *bye, yes* and *no*).

Characteristics of Intermediate Words

Great sets of additional vocabulary consist of words that . . .

Offer Potential for Combining

If your dog hasn't begun combining words yet, they likely will in this stage of learning! Having a variety of verbs, adjectives, and nouns can help ensure your dog can create combinations that make sense.

Can Be Used for Purposes Other Than Requesting

In the coming chapters, you'll learn all about ways your dog may use words other than requesting. Selecting a variety of word types gives your dog the opportunity to communicate for different reasons.

Fill Any Communication Gaps You've Encountered Throughout Your Teaching

Now that both you and your dog have a foundation in button communication, have you noticed times where your dog is trying to communicate something they don't have a word for or times when you've wanted to model a word that you don't have a button for? This is a great time to fill those gaps.

Expand On What Your Dog Loves to Communicate About

Since you've likely introduced a variety of topics to your dog, now you can choose words that expand on what they like to talk about most. For example, if your dog loves communicating about going outside, you could add a couple more words to represent their favorite places or activities.

Putting It All Together

With the above characteristics in mind, look at the beginner (see page 34) and intermediate sections (see below) of the vocabulary index. When you see words you're interested in adding, write them down below in the space provided and include when you could model them, too. Thinking ahead about when and how to model words helps us all make choices that would be beneficial for our pups. Don't worry about writing too many choices down. In the activities at the end of the chapter, we'll make a plan for introducing them.

POPULAR INTERMEDIATE CORE WORDS	WHY THEY WORK
Help	*Help* is a versatile word with a lot of potential. Whether it's to retrieve a toy stuck under the couch or to alert you of a more serious problem, all dogs will need help at some point in time.
Look	Dogs often want to draw our attention toward them or toward something they notice in their surroundings. *Look* is a way your dog can communicate this desire for connection clearly to you, and pair it with what they want you to look at.
Want	We are constantly asking our dogs "What do you want?" when we notice them communicating in any way to us. *Want* can help your dog learn to combine words and eventually to distinguish between a desire and an observation.
Good	We say "good girl" or "good boy" all the time when we're proud of our dogs! *Good* gives your dog the opportunity to tell you when they're proud or extra happy with what's going on.
Yes	*Yes* is a common response when your dog does something you're proud of, or when you're saying yes to a request. *Yes* gives your pup a way to validate what they want and affirm what you're doing.
No	We all deserve the power to say no. If we're telling our dogs no to teach them what not to do, our dogs should have a way to tell us the same thing if we're doing something they don't like. *No* can also serve as the absence of an activity (e.g., *No eat, no park*).

POPULAR INTERMEDIATE FRINGE WORDS	WHY THEY WORK
Dog's name	Your dog knows their name and can use it to talk about what they want or what they're doing.
Your name and the names of other family members	Your dog may want someone specific in your household for certain activities or may share that they're thinking about you while you're gone. Dogs are pack animals who care deeply about their family.
The names of other pets	Dogs have relationships with and thoughts about the other animals who share their home, too. Talking about what other pets are doing is great for modeling and showing your dog how they can comment on their environment.
Inside or *Home*	These words can be used to talk about when you're staying in vs. going out, and will allow your pup to communicate about their environment more clearly.
Puzzle (or other specific activity name)	If a special toy or activity is part of your dog's regular routine, they should have a way to talk about it. We all talk about the things we love, dogs included!

POPULAR INTERMEDIATE FRINGE WORDS	WHY THEY WORK
Locations your dog likes to visit	Maybe it's the dog park, a friend's house, Starbucks, or the local pet shop. Giving your dog a way to say specific locations allows you to understand exactly where they're thinking about or wanting to visit.

Words I'm Interested in Adding

WORD	WHEN I COULD MODEL IT

Setup

As we learned in chapter 4, it's extremely important to keep your dog's buttons in the same spots. Your dog memorizes the location of each button, similar to how we learn where each letter on the QWERTY keyboard is through typing practice and develop muscle memory for each key. This means that when you add buttons to your dog's vocabulary, you should keep all your original words in their same spots.

If all your buttons are in one central location on a mat, use the following guidance on how to expand:

- Add another mat next to or below your current button mat. If you're using mats that attach together, you can even add the next mat before you add the buttons. This can help get your dog used to walking on and through their mat to access all the words.
- Most button mats fit two rows of buttons (top and bottom). Add your new mat(s) next to your current mat on the right side if you want to keep all your buttons as outer row buttons. This setup works well for dogs who don't walk through their mats or reach over buttons to access words in the top row.
- If your dog does walk through their mat(s) or easily reaches across their mat to access different words, you can add your new mat either next to or below your current mat.

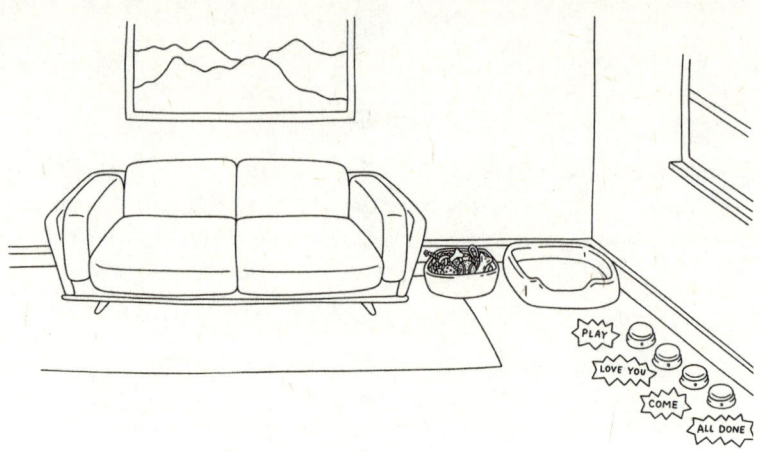

If your buttons are located in different areas of your home, use the following guidance on how to expand:

- If you're adding words that are representative of specific activities, you can place the button near where the activity happens just as you did with your beginning words.
- If you're adding more abstract words, you can place your buttons along a wall in your living room or other high-traffic areas of your home.
- It's okay to have multiple buttons in the same area. For example, you might have both *outside* and *walk* near the door, and have words like *play, come, love you,* and *all done* lined up against the wall of your living room. This can be a great way to introduce the concept of having multiple words in the same location. Just make sure to keep them in the same order! If you transition to keeping your buttons in one central location someday, your dog will already have practice with finding the button they're looking for in an array of multiple options before them.

Activities

1. Communication Detective 2.0

Now that you've been teaching words, you're likely even more observant of all your dog's forms of communication. Can you think of any times of the day or situations where your dog is using gestures, body language, or vocalizations to communicate something to you? You can use this information to help you make decisions about which words to add next.

EXAMPLES

I realized that . . . *my dog looks up to the cabinet where I keep their dental bones every evening.*
What they're trying to communicate: *They want me to get them a dental bone.*
Words I could teach: *want, bone, Greenie*

I realized that . . . *my dog whines and tries to get me to go upstairs every night.*
What they're trying to communicate: *They're ready to go to bed.*
Words I could teach: *bed, all done, want, upstairs*

Your turn!

I REALIZED THAT . . .

My dog_____ when _____.
What they're trying to communicate:
Words I could teach:

My dog_____ when _____.
What they're trying to communicate:
Words I could teach:

My dog_____ when _____.
What they're trying to communicate:
Words I could teach:

My dog_____ when _____.
What they're trying to communicate:
Words I could teach:

My dog_____ when _____.
What they're trying to communicate:
Words I could teach:

2. Plan Your Lineup

Each time you're ready to add new words, take a look at the list you created earlier in this chapter of words you're interested in, and the activity you completed above.

Pick two to four words that are the highest priority for you now. High-priority words are often those that you find yourself wanting to model throughout the day but don't have a button for, that your dog is trying to communicate via other forms of communication, or that you think would help fill a communication gap you're experiencing with your dog. These are your up-to-bat buttons.

Pick another two to four words that are a mid-level priority for you right now. Mid-level-priority words are often words that would allow your dog to get more specific in their communication or expand on their interests. These are your on-deck buttons. Add these two to four weeks after your up-to-bat words.

UP-TO-BAT WORDS

_____

_____

_____

ON-DECK WORDS

_____

_____

_____

Summary

When adding more words, choose vocabulary that you can use for different purposes. Intermediate words can be more abstract than beginner words. Add two to four words at a time, and allow two to four weeks for you to teach and for your dog to practice with them before introducing more.

CHAPTER 10

Generalizing Skills

While my husband and I were out of town, we received the following text from my mother-in-law, who was watching Stella:

At 2:30 AM I needed to get some hot tea. Stella got up with me . . . she said "Park outside." I answered "No outside." She answered "Mad want outside." I took her out and she went potty and pooped three times. Thank God for buttons!!!

This interaction between Stella and my mother-in-law is an example of Stella's *generalization,* the ability to demonstrate a skill in an environment different from the one a learner was taught in. The concept of generalization is one of the areas where traditional dog training methods and teaching button communication overlap. According to *Whole Dog Journal,* preparing your dog to generalize a skill means "practicing with your dog in different places, at different times of the day, under different conditions, in the presence of different people, dogs, and a variety of other distractions."

From the time when Stella was a young puppy with only a few words in her vocabulary, I knew I wanted her to be able to use buttons with anyone who was with her, not just with me. This skill would be the marker of true independent communication, not a trick or response to a command that only I signaled.

Plus, I wanted Stella's thoughts to be acknowledged and her needs met no matter who was caring for her. The ways I taught Stella from her early days with buttons enabled her to develop the skills to communicate so directly in the middle of the night, with someone other than her primary caregivers, in a different environment.

Now that you've introduced buttons to your dog and have seen success with at least a few words, you can start preparing your dog to be able to generalize their communication, too. When and how you model words can set your pup up for long-term communication success, no matter who they are with or what's going on around them!

How We All Learn Skills

The process of generalization occurs in humans, too, not just in dogs. It's how we all learn many skills: first in a controlled environment, then generalized to the real world over time. For example, the first time I tried driving a car, I was with my mom in a very large, empty parking lot. The radio was turned off, there weren't any other cars around, and there was nobody else in our vehicle to distract me. This controlled environment provided me with the opportunity to focus, learn the skills I needed, and practice getting a feel for driving. Once I got the hang of driving in an empty parking lot, we moved to quiet streets, then to roads through town, and eventually to the highway. As driving became more automatic, we increased the complexity of the environment by adding other passengers, music, driving at different times of the day, and so forth.

Our dogs need practice generalizing skills as well. Even though your buttons are set up in your home, it's great to get your dog accustomed to using them when they stay overnight somewhere else, have guests over, or have a sitter staying with them. This ensures that your dog will be able to share what's on their mind no matter who is caring for them.

How to Practice Generalization with Your Dog

As I mentioned in the introduction, preparing your dog to generalize a skill means "practicing with your dog in different places, at different times of the day, under different conditions, in the presence of different people, dogs, and a variety of other distractions." Here's what you can do to promote generalization of words:

Use Your Dog's Buttons . . .

In Different Places

- If you use a button mat with all your buttons together, try taking the mat into different areas of your home. If you and your dog will be hanging out in your room together for the next couple of hours, take the buttons with you. This helps your dog learn that their words are available to them anywhere, and that they can talk no matter what's going on.
- Next time you take a trip with your dog, pack up your buttons, too! See "Travel with Your Buttons" below for more travel tips.
- When your dog stays overnight at a sitter's house, take their buttons with them. Show your sitter how they can model words and how they can respond if your dog says something.

At Different Times of the Day

- Model words in short bursts throughout the day rather than during one long modeling session each day. Remember, frequency of modeling is more important than duration of modeling!
- Practice using words in new ways. Pick a couple of your vocabulary words and see if you can brainstorm other times of day when they would be relevant. For example, instead of modeling *bed* only at night before going to bed, you could model it in the morning by saying "All done bed." We'll dive deeper into this in chapter 10.

Under Different Conditions

- Typically dogs learn to use buttons first when they're calm and focused. Start modeling words when you notice your dog in a more heightened state, too. Maybe your dog saw a squirrel out the window, heard a car pull up in the driveway, or has the zoomies after their bath. Model a relevant word or two during these times, too, so your dog learns that they can use their buttons even when they're more amped up.

In the Presence of Different People, Dogs, and a Variety of Other Distractions

- See "The More the Merrier" below for details on how to involve others in your teaching.
- Bring your environment back to normal. If you've kept the area around your buttons calm and quiet when you're teaching, start introducing some more distractions. You can turn music or the TV on, talk on the phone, or have conversations with family members around your dog's buttons. Stop what you're doing intermittently to model a word, so your dog learns how to focus on their buttons even when there are other distractions happening around them.

Activities to Promote Generalization

1. The More the Merrier

To help your dog learn how to use their words with other people, it's important to give others the opportunity to use their words, too!

When you have visitors over, show them your dog's buttons! If they're interacting with your dog, encourage them to say a word like *play* or *love you*. Before they leave, have them say *bye* using your dog's buttons.

If you live with family members or friends, ask them to model words for your dog. As with any training or teaching, it's important to have consistency across a household. Even if you're the primary teacher, your dog will benefit from seeing others interact with their buttons as well. Here are some ways you can include the members of your household in the process:

Designate routines to certain people.

Who is the one to wake up first and feed your dog or take them outside? Who usually takes your dog for a walk? Who leaves for work every day? Who gets their special dental treat out at dinner time? Whoever is in charge of routines can be in charge of modeling a word that goes with the routine. Giving your family members a specific word or two to focus on can increase the likelihood that they'll participate consistently.

Involve your children.

Teaching your dog to talk is a great activity for children of all ages to be included in. The whole experience can open up opportunities for talking to children about the ways our pets communicate, listening to their voices, and tools that help humans communicate, too. Here are a few tips for including your children in your teaching at each age:

Babies and Toddlers

- If you model words for your dog, your baby or toddler will see this and learn how to push the buttons, too.
- Say things like "This is how Stella talks" or "These are Stella's words" from an early age. Your little one is understanding more than you think. By talking about the purpose of the buttons, you are preparing for when your child can interact with them more.
- Let your little one explore the buttons in a controlled environment. Say the words back to them that they're pressing. If your dog might react strongly to this, it may be best to let your child explore when your dog is outside or busy with something else. If your child starts being too rambunctious with the buttons, gently redirect them to another activity and put the buttons back where they belong.

Young Children

- Kids love when they can help out in a special way. Give your young child the "job" of pressing a couple of your dog's buttons before certain activities.
- Teach your child how to wait for your dog to respond. Practice counting to 10 or 20 quietly after your child models a word. This shows your child the power of patience and gives your dog a chance to respond.
- Take turns modeling. You can start by saying, "Mom's turn to press Stella's button!" (Press the button.) Then you can say, "[Your child's name's] turn to press Stella's button!" (Give them the chance to press the button.)

Middle and High Schoolers

- Older kids and teenagers can really take an active role in teaching their dog to talk. I've worked with multiple students who have successfully taught their dog a few words for school projects. Allow your child to pick words they think your dog would want to say and take the lead on teaching those concepts.
- Talk with your child about how teaching and training take time. This will help them understand the importance of consistency and patience.
- Talk to your child about signs of progress they can look for (chapter 6, page 59). You can follow along with your dog's advancement using a tracker, such as our Hunger for Words Talking Pet Goal Tracker, to take note of the words your child is teaching and signs of progress.

2. Travel with Your Buttons

If you're traveling with your dog, try taking their buttons when possible! New environments give your dog the opportunity to use words in new ways. Every time I've taken Stella's buttons with us on a trip, she has created unique word combinations or surprised me with what she's thinking about. Here are a few tips for traveling with your buttons:

Keep your setup consistent.

Your dog is learning or has learned the location of each of their words. If you keep your buttons in a mat, take the buttons and mat with you to keep everything in the same places. If you keep your buttons in different areas of your home, try your best to replicate this setup wherever you're staying (for example, *outside* button near the door, *eat* button near the food dish, *play* button near toys, and so forth).

Take a few moments to model your dog's words when you get them set up.

Show your dog that their words are the same by modeling each of them when you get settled in where you're staying. This is especially important if you don't keep your buttons in a mat because the locations will likely be a little different from your home.

Provide some extra modeling and teaching support.
Your dog is used to using their buttons at home, not necessarily in other places. On the first couple of trips you take with your dog and their buttons, be prepared to model words a little more than you do at home or to give more cues than you use at home. This will help your dog learn that their buttons are a tool for them to use anywhere they are and will strengthen their independence with them.

Summary

In order for your dog to use their buttons in any context no matter who is caring for them, they'll need practice generalizing their skills. By including others in your teaching, bringing buttons with your dog when they stay somewhere else, and modeling words in lots of different situations, you are setting your dog up for long-term success.

CHAPTER 11
Using Words for Different Reasons

When Stella was a young puppy with only three words in her vocabulary, she said something one morning that made me question everything about dogs' potential for learning and sharing language.

I was in the sunroom watering my plants while Stella stood behind me, watching as usual. She was like my little shadow, always interested in what I was doing and eager to participate in some way. But this time, in the middle of my watering, Stella abruptly turned around and left the room.

"Water," I heard from her button ten seconds later.

Hmm, her water dish must be empty, I thought. *Maybe seeing the water reminded her that she was thirsty.* At this point in my teaching, I had modeled *water* only when Stella was getting a drink or when I noticed that her bowl was empty.

I walked into the dining room, expecting to fill up her bowl. Instead, I saw a full water dish and watched Stella walk back into the sunroom without taking a drink. She continued watching me water the plants until I finished.

Once I processed what just happened, it didn't take long for my speech therapist brain to kick into action. Stella just used a word (*water*) in a way that I had never modeled before. That meant Stella was taking the words I was teaching her and applying them to new circumstances all on her own. Even more impressive to me was that Stella used her *water* button to share an observation rather than to tell me she needed water. This was the first time that Stella's communication wasn't transactional. Stella wasn't using a button to receive something from me; instead, she was using her buttons to connect with me.

As a speech therapist, I am well versed in all the reasons why a child might say a word other than requesting something. It is an important part of my job to make sure kids who used communication devices had access to vocabulary that would allow them to talk in the same ways as their peers, even if it is through a different modality. But truthfully, I had never expected Stella to develop this ability to use words in different ways, for different reasons.

Over the subsequent months and years, I monitored Stella's word use, modeled words in new ways, and tested new categories of vocabulary. I've found that Stella (and other dogs) use words for six overall functions of communication, just as young children do.

What Are Communication Functions?

Up until this point of the book, we've focused primarily on teaching your dog to use words to tell you what they need or want. This is the most straight-forward and expected reason for communicating—to request an object, person, or action. But there are many other reasons your dog may want to communicate with you, too! All of these different reasons are known as *communication functions*.

After dogs use words to request, they often start using those same words for different reasons, just like the example in the introduction of Stella saying *water* to label what I was doing: watering my plants. Without having background knowledge of different communication functions and what to look for, this stage can be confusing for many pet parents. Their dogs might have been using words in expected ways and contexts up until now. Suddenly dogs are saying words at new times when they don't need something. This often leaves pet parents wondering if their dog really understands the words they're saying.

By learning what the overall functions of communication are, how you can recognize them, and how you can support them, you'll be equipped to encourage their development and spot different functions when they occur.

The six overall functions of communication are *requesting, protesting, describing, commenting, asking / answering questions,* and *expressing feelings.* In this intermediate stage of learning, you can expect to see your dog using words to request, protest, describe, and comment. We'll focus on the last two communication functions in the advanced section of this guidebook (see page 140).

Requesting

What This Means

Your dog is telling you what they want or need. Your dog will demonstrate requesting in their beginning stage of learning, but may progress to using multiword combinations to make requests during this intermediate stage. Your dog may request an object (e.g., *ball*), action (e.g., *play*), person (e.g., *Mom*), place (e.g., *park*), or activity (e.g., *walk*).

Characteristics

You can recognize requesting when your dog uses a word around the time when an activity would typically be taking place. For example, your dog might say *outside* first thing in the morning after waking up or may say *eat* at 5:00 p.m. when you would normally be feeding them. Other signs of requesting include your dog's using a word before or after they've used another form of communication. For example, your dog might say *play*, then bow to you to signal playtime, or might say *bed* after whining at the bottom of the stairs at night.

Words to Model

You can model action words, objects, names, and locations as they're happening or right before they will take place. This teaches your dog which words symbolize specific activities and shows her how she can ask for something when she wants or needs it.

As you increase your dog's vocabulary and start working on word combinations, you can model the word *want* as well. As you recognize your dog making a request (such as to go outside), you can say and model *want outside*. This will help you and your dog differentiate between requests and other purposes for communicating.

How You Can Support It

All of the strategies we discussed in Part One will help your dog learn to request. By narrating your dog's actions and labeling their desires, you are teaching your dog how to make requests using words.

Protesting

What This Means

Your dog is rejecting an object, activity, or direction you give.

Characteristics

You may observe this function first through your dog's body language. If you call your dog over and they stay where they are, if they walk away from their food after you feed them, or if they walk in the opposite direction of where you're trying to direct them, your dog is protesting.

You can recognize protesting with words when your dog says *all done* or *no*. You may be working longer than usual and hear your dog say *all done* or your dog might run away and say *no* when she sees you get the nail clippers out.

Words to Model

You can model *all done* or *no* when you see your dog protesting with their body language as described above. You can also model *no* if your dog is doing something you don't want them to be doing. This teaches your dog how they can tell you *no* if you're doing something they don't like or want.

How You Can Support It

Listen to and respect your dog's opinions. Remember, your dog doesn't have to say *yes* to everything you suggest. When you allow your dog the opportunity to say *no* and listen when they say it, you are showing that their opinions matter and that they can trust you when they share something. If your dog says *no* to something they have to do right now, try acknowledging their message first, then giving them more support through it. For example, one day when I was getting ready to leave for work, I told Stella it was time for her to lie in her bed. Instead of moving, she said *bye no* and stayed right where she was. It wasn't an option for me to stay home with her, but I recognized that she was having a hard time with me leaving. I first acknowledged her message by recasting it back to her: *Stella no want Christina bye.* Then I provided more support: *Love you Stella,* I said. *Christina come later.* I gave her lots of belly rubs and spent a few extra dedicated moments with her before heading out for the day.

Describing

What This Means

Your dog is labeling something they observe in their environment, narrating what's going on around them, or giving more details about a request.

Characteristics

Your dog may say a word for something they see or identify (like the *water* example from the introduction to this chapter) or talk about what you're doing (like saying *Mom bye* as you're getting ready to leave for work). Your dog might also share information about what they just did (like saying *play park* when returning from the park, or *all done eat* after finishing their meal). They are describing what happened or is currently happening to you.

Words to Model

Model your current vocabulary in new circumstances. For example, instead of modeling *outside* only when your dog is requesting to go out, you can model *all done outside* when she comes back in, model *water outside* if it's raining, or *Mom outside* if you pop out to get the mail or take the garbage out. This will help your dog see that they can use words to make observations and talk about what's happening rather than just when making requests.

How You Can Support It

Validate your dog's observations and narrations to you. You can respond with a simple yes or you can repeat their message back to them when your dog talks about what they're noticing. This communication function is especially popular with young toddlers. If you've spent time with a one- or two-year-old, you can probably think of a time when they just pointed out everything they saw in their environment to you. All you had to do was say, "Yes, that's blue," or "Yes, that's a bus," to validate their message. It's the same concept here.

Commenting

What This Means

Your dog is expressing an opinion about something or using words for social purposes.

Characteristics

Your dog may say *Love you Mom* after you give her lots of belly rubs or *good eat* after having an especially delicious dinner; she may comment on the absence of a typical activity such as *no walk* if you skipped your typical walk. This is very similar to the describing function. But instead of purely narrating what happened, your dog is providing an additional thought or detail about her experience.

Words to Model

You can model *good* when you're proud of your dog or when she does something well. This will teach her how she can say when she thinks something is good, too. You can model *no good* or add a word like *bad* to model when it seems like your dog really doesn't like something. If you don't want to add simple adjectives, you can model *love you* or *yes* as a replacement instead. When you're proud of your dog, you can say *Yes Stella* or *Love you Stella*. If you just finished an especially fun play session with your dog, you could comment *love you play*.

How You Can Support It

Model your own descriptions to your dog. If you had a lot of fun with them, tell them with their buttons! If you notice something missing from your routine, call it out. You can respond to your dog's comments by validating their message, just as we discussed in the describing section above.

Differentiating Between Functions

If you're not sure whether your dog was making a request or using their words for a different purpose, consider these three function factors:

Context / Environment

What's happening around you or your dog right now? Could their words describe something they're seeing or hearing in the environment?

Your dog's body language

Is your dog more relaxed or uptight? More relaxed states generally correlate with commenting or describing, whereas more uptight states usually indicate a need, a want, or a more intense emotion.

Your dog's reaction to your response

If you respond by validating your dog's message, do they seem content? Or do they try saying the word again or in a different way? If your dog does not seem content with your simply acknowledging what they said, that typically indicates a need or want rather than a comment or description.

Activities

Model your dog's original words in one new context each day.

In the chart below, write down your dog's original buttons and one new context (that isn't requesting) where you could model word(s) for them. Aim to model at least one new context each day. If you need help thinking of new contexts, use the functions list from earlier in the chapter or the examples below to get ideas.

Example:

WORD	NEW CONTEXT IDEAS
Eat	I could model *eat* while I'm eating, *all done eat* when I finish eating, and *eat* when I'm putting my son in his high chair
Play	I could model *play* when I notice Stella chewing on a toy to comment on what she's doing, *all done play* when we return from the park, or *play eat* when I introduce a new puzzle toy to Stella
Outside	I could model *outside* when I go outside to get the mail, when I see Stella looking out the window, or when we hear loud noises outside
Walk	I could model *all done walk* when we come back from a walk, or *walk water outside* if we're going for a walk in the rain
Love You	I could model *love you* when I hug my husband, when my son gently pets Stella, or when one of Stella's favorite people comes to visit
WORD	NEW CONTEXT IDEAS
Water	I could model *water* when I'm filling up my own water bottle, watering my plants, or *all done water* when I finish giving Stella a bath

Your turn!

WORD	NEW CONTEXT IDEAS

Summary

We all communicate for different purposes, dogs included! The first reasons your dog will likely use words other than to *request* are to *protest, describe,* and *comment.* The context, your dog's body language, and your dog's response to your response will help you distinguish between functions. Model using your dog's buttons in different ways to help show your dog all the different ways they can use words, too.

CHAPTER 12

Combining Words

As I sat on the couch chatting with my sister on the phone, Stella stood right at my feet staring up to me.

"Uh-huh," I said to my sister. "Sounds good."

Stella walked to her buttons. *Look come play,* she said.

I smiled and picked up a ball from Stella's toy bin. "Here you go, girl," I whispered before bouncing the ball for her.

Stella paced back and forth across the living room before returning to her buttons. *Want play outside*, she said. Stella didn't want to play with the ball, she wanted to go play outside together.

I turned the phone away from my face. "Play outside later, Stella," I quickly said before putting it back to my ear.

Stella huffed and whined. *Want play outside*, she repeated.

"Sorry, Stella keeps trying to get me to play outside," I said to my sister. "Not now, Stella. Play when I'm all done," I said.

I walked into the next room, hoping Stella would follow. But instead, she stayed right next to her words.

No play outside, she commented.

"That's right, Stella. No play now. I'm on the phone," I said over my shoulder.

My sister and I continued chatting for a few more minutes. I returned to the living room, where I saw Stella sitting next to her button board like she was waiting to have a word with me. Stella stood up and slammed on two buttons that would break my heart.

Love you no, she said.

This interaction is bursting with multi-word combinations and different communication functions. Even though Stella used only six different buttons throughout this entire exchange, she combined them together in different ways to create different meanings. Being able to put words together in unique ways and create entirely new meanings each time is the incredible power of language.

When I first introduced buttons to Stella, I had no idea that she would reach this stage of language development. Stella began by combining two words together, then increased to three-, four-, and eventually five- and six-word combinations. In the years since our work became public, thousands of other dogs have progressed to this level as well, showing that dogs have incredible potential when given the opportunity to learn.

In this chapter, we're going to focus on helping your dog create two-word phrases and helping you interpret those phrases when you hear them. Then in Part Three of this book, we'll move on to more complex phrases and short sentences.

Quick Vocabulary and Setup Check

Getting to the stage of combining words presents a great opportunity to evaluate your vocabulary. Are you able to combine words easily to make phrases with the buttons your dog has available? If not, it may be time to add new words. Having a variety of core words (verbs and adjectives) can help you create meaningful combinations. If your dog's vocabulary is mostly nouns, take a look at the Popular Beginning Core Words chart (see pages 33–34) for ideas on which words to add.

Additionally, this is an excellent time to evaluate your dog's current setup. If you began with buttons placed in different areas of your home, your dog beginning to combine words or showing signs of combining words is the time to transition to one central location. Visit chapter 4 (see page 39), for more information on how to do this successfully.

When to Expect Word Combinations

In typical language development, babies and toddlers use gestures and sounds to communicate single words, then two-word phrases, and finally three-plus-word phrases and sentences. Children spend time in each stage practicing their skills and developing before moving on to higher levels of complexity.

Dogs go through similar progressions when learning to talk. Typically, dogs don't immediately start combining words intentionally, just as toddlers rarely start communicating in phrases and short sentences as soon as they learn to say words. Some dogs learn to combine words quickly, just weeks after starting to say words, whereas other dogs take longer to reach this stage of communication. In my experience, adult dogs are more likely to combine words quicker than puppies because they have been hearing you talk for years. They have more experience with hearing different phrases and sentences and understanding what they mean than puppies do.

Three Signs Your Dog Is Ready to Combine Words

1. Your dog independently uses single words multiple times each day.

The more practice your dog has with their buttons, the more likely they are to learn how to combine words and make short phrases. When the buttons have become an important and commonplace tool for them to express themselves, they will be motivated to try saying more with their words and creating unique phrases.

2. Your dog uses words for multiple purposes.

Combining words to make phrases requires your dog to have the understanding that words can be used in different ways. When you've seen your dog generalize words and use words for multiple functions of communication, they are most likely on the verge of putting words together themselves.

3. Your dog combines a word and a gesture.

Gestures for concepts often develop before the words do. If your dog is combining a word and a gesture, that typically comes before combining two words together.

Examples

- Your dog says *outside* and circles around you, herding you out the door when they're trying to get you to come out with them. You may notice this before your dog learns to say *come outside* or *Mom outside*.
- Your dog says *eat* and paws at their empty treat ball. You may notice this before they learn to say *play eat* or *ball eat*.

When you observe these skills, complete the activities below with your dog to help them reach this exciting next stage of learning!

Activities to Promote Word Combinations

1. Recasting

When your dog says a single word, repeat the word back to them and add another word before or after it. For example, if your dog says *outside*, you can use your dog's buttons and your verbal speech to say something like *yes outside, play outside, Stella outside, come outside.*

By doing this, you are modeling the next level of development for your dog and showing how they can put words together themselves. For best results, keep your responses varied. This will help your dog see how they can use words in many different combinations.

SELF-TALK

PARALLEL TALK

2. Operation Narration 2.0

Back in chapter 2 (page 19), we learned how to implement Operation Narration: using words to label your dog's actions. Now that your dog is starting to combine words, we can ramp up the narration again and label what's happening in new ways.

Take a look at the chart on page 128 to learn how to narrate what you're doing and what your dog is doing with different phrases. Try using both of these types of narration at least twice per day with your dog's buttons.

TYPE OF NARRATION	WHAT IT MEANS	EXAMPLES
Self-talk	Using your dog's buttons to describe what you're doing	Telling Stella . . . *Christina bed* when I'm going up to bed *Christina look* when I'm looking at Stella *Come outside* before I take Stella out *Christina eat* when I'm eating *Christina all done* when I finish working
Parallel talk	Using your dog's buttons to describe what your dog or another person is doing	Saying . . . *Stella play* when Stella grabs a toy *Bye Stella* when she walks into another room *Jake bye* when my husband Jake leaves *Want walk* when Stella waits in front of the door *Look outside* when Stella is looking out the window

3. Pump Up the Pause Time

Back when you were first introducing words to your dog, you learned how to add pause time within your interactions. Increased pause time helped your dog learn when it was their turn to talk and gave them enough time to process what was happening and try something new.

When your dog is in the middle of developing a new skill (such as combining words), they will likely need this support again. When you see your dog start to combine words or when you've been modeling word combinations for a few weeks, try this:

> *After your dog says a single word, stay quiet for fifteen to twenty seconds.* You've likely gotten into the habit of responding to your dog's words right away, which is great! But now take a step back and give your dog time to potentially add another word onto their message.
>
> If after fifteen to twenty seconds your dog hasn't added a word and doesn't seem like they're going to, you can recast your dog's production (see Activity 1 on page 127). Continue giving your dog this pause time and modeling two-word phrases a few times each day.

Understanding Your Dog's Word Combinations

Word combinations can help your dog become even clearer and more specific in their communication. As we learned in chapter 10, your dog can use words for a variety of purposes. Some common reasons your dog may combine words together include:

- Making a new request (e.g., *Look outside* to request opening the blinds and looking out the window)
- Making a more detailed request (e.g., *Play puzzle* to request specifically what to play with)
- Describing what's happening around them (e.g., *Mom eat* when you're cooking or eating)
- Creating a phrase for a concept they don't have a button for (e.g., *Water play* to talk about the beach or a pool)

Babbling or Intentional?

Sometimes it can be difficult to tell whether your dog is babbling and exploring their buttons or making a meaningful phrase. Whether it was intentional or not, responding to your dog's phrase as if it was meaningful will help them learn the meaning of different words combined together. With that being said, it's helpful to understand if your dog is at the stage of making intentional phrases or not, so you know what level of support they need from you as a teacher. Take a look at the lists below to help you assess your dog's phrases.

Indicators That Your Dog Is Babbling / Exploring

- You haven't observed any of the "Three Signs Your Dog Is Ready to Combine Words" (see page 125).
- Your dog quickly pushes multiple buttons without really looking.
- Your dog is an exploratory learner (see page 60) who is newer to buttons.
- Your dog only ever pushes multiple buttons that are right next to each other.
- You don't ever hear the phrase again.

Indicators That Your Dog Created a Phrase Intentionally

- You've observed the "Three Signs Your Dog Is Ready to Combine Words" (see page 125).
- Your dog looks at what they're pressing.
- Your dog combines words that aren't right next to each other.
- Your dog frequently combines the same words.

What to Do If . . .

Your Dog Consistently Uses a Phrase That You Don't Understand

When anyone (human or animal) is in the earlier stages of language development or has a more limited vocabulary, there will be times of confusion or misunderstanding. Language is subjective. We often use words that we specifically associate with an object or experience that another person doesn't necessarily share. For example, whenever my one-year-old son holds up a black crayon, he says "Maisie," the name of my parents' dog, who happens to be black. A stranger would not understand this connection, but someone with context (his family) does. The same goes for Stella. When she sees us getting ready to leave, she says *bye eat* anticipating the Kong we fill with peanut butter. Without knowing that routine, a stranger would probably have a hard time understanding what she meant.

Repetition typically indicates intention. If your dog creates a phrase that doesn't seem to make sense once and you never hear it again, they were probably exploring their words or just made a mistake. But if your dog uses the same phrase multiple times, there's likely a reason behind it even if you're not sure what that reason is at first. Use the following questions to help you get to the bottom of what they're saying:

- What's going on around your dog right now? Could they be talking about something they're seeing, hearing, or smelling?
- Is there a routine activity coming up? Could they be talking about something that's about to happen?
- Is your dog using any other forms of communication? Are they walking to a certain area, whining, or looking somewhere specific?
- Could your dog be combining words to create a phrase for a concept they don't have a word for?
- Does your dog try saying anything else if you don't respond?

Summary

Combining words together to create short phrases and sentences is an incredible milestone for your dog to reach. Word combinations typically occur when your dog is using single words independently, for different reasons, and consistently. Model short phrases with your dog's buttons to show them how they can put words together, too.

PART THREE

ADVANCED LEARNERS

Signs Your Dog Is an Advanced Learner

- Your dog uses ten plus words to communicate independently.
- Your dog combines words together multiple times per day.
- Your dog uses words for reasons other than requesting.
- Your dog uses their buttons with other people in your home and in different contexts in your home.

CHAPTER 13

Teaching Advanced Concepts

One day on our typical morning walk around the park, there was a squirrel on the other side of the fence taunting Stella. The squirrel chattered at her and ran up and down the fence, continuously teasing her.

Stella pawed at the fence, barked, ran along the fence, but nothing she did got the squirrel to stop.

When we returned home from the walk twenty minutes later, Stella marched straight to her button board and slammed her paw on two buttons: *Mad park*.

About thirty seconds later, she said *Mad mad* again.

Stella's words on this day fascinated me because they showed how long she was thinking about an event that frustrated her. Without her buttons, I would never have known that the squirrel from the park was still on Stella's mind. And I definitely wouldn't have realized just how mad it made her!

Growing your dog's vocabulary to include advanced concepts such as emotion words, simple time words, and other complex concepts gives your dog the power to express deeper thoughts and gives you the opportunity to understand your dog's behavior and mind from a different perspective.

When to Grow Your Vocabulary

At this stage of learning, your dog is using their buttons every day and saying words in unique ways. Oftentimes, this is when pet parents are most shocked by their pup's intelligence, skills, and potential. When buttons have become an indispensable tool for your dog, you can add and teach more advanced concepts. Words in this stage can be more abstract, as you have more experience teaching, your dog has a solid understanding of how to use buttons, and your dog is communicating in more sophisticated ways. Follow your dog's lead: when they're an eager learner and communicator, give them more to talk about!

Below are the "Five Indicators That Your Dog Is Ready for More Words" from chapter 9 (see page 94), updated to reflect this advanced stage of learning.

Five Indicators That Your Dog Is Ready for More Words

1. They use all or most of their vocabulary.

The most obvious sign that your dog is ready for more words is when they have used all or most of their buttons intentionally. The only way for your dog to learn how to say new words is to have new words available to them. This means that when you're actively teaching your pup, you should always have at least a couple of words that they're still learning.

2. They make word combinations daily.

If your dog is creating phrases and short sentences with the words they have available, they are likely ready for more words. They may be combining words together to create phrases for concepts they don't have a button for. This is perfectly normal and a great skill! Support their desire to talk about more by adding more words.

3. They seem frustrated around their buttons (whining, pawing around at several buttons when trying to get your attention).

This is another key indicator that your dog is trying to say something but doesn't have the word available. If you have some idea about what they might be trying to tell you based on what's happening and their other forms of communication, introduce a word for that concept and try modeling it.

4. They are using their basic words in more advanced ways.

As we learned in chapter 10, your dog can use words for different purposes. When you see your dog using even the most basic words in unique and creative ways, or to talk about more complex situations, they are definitely ready for more advanced concepts.

5. They're going through times of transition.

Maybe you're moving, welcoming a new baby, visiting a new park semi-regularly, or bringing your dog to daycare a few times a week. As always, new routines warrant new words!

What Are Advanced Concepts and When Is My Dog Ready for Them?

ADVANCED CONCEPT	VOCABULARY IDEAS	WHY THEY WORK	SIGNS YOUR DOG IS READY
Emotions	*Happy* *Mad* *Sad* *Scared* *Upset*	Dogs are emotional beings. They demonstrate different emotions with their body language and vocalizations. By pairing words to what you're observing, you can help your dog communicate more about what's making her feel certain ways.	• *Your dog expresses a couple of simple emotions through their body language that you understand.* • *Your dog uses words for different functions, and is starting to make more comments / observations.* • *You're often wondering why your dog is upset.*
Time	*Now* *Soon* *Later*	Dogs have an excellent internal clock. They anticipate routine events and daily activities. Using simple time concepts, you and your dog can talk about what's happening now vs. what's happening later on in the day.	• *Your dog starts talking about things that have just happened or will happen later.* • *Your dog lists sequences of events.* • *Your dog consistently combines words together. These words are difficult to understand on their own.*

ADVANCED CONCEPT	VOCABULARY IDEAS	WHY THEY WORK	SIGNS YOUR DOG IS READY
Question Words	*Where?* *What?* *Who?* *When?*	We ask our dogs questions such as "What do you want?" "Where's your ball?" "Who's here?" all of the time. Your dog has likely heard you use these question words and has been responding either with their gestures or with a word. Your dog can ask simple questions, too, when they're wondering what's going to happen.	• *Your dog likes when you tell them where you're going, who you're seeing, what you'll be doing, etc.* • *Your dog looks for specific objects or people around your home.* • *Your dog is regularly combining words and engaging in short conversations with you.*
Body Parts	*Ears* *Belly* *Back* *Paw* *Mouth*	Labeling your dog's body parts can help them tell you if there's something wrong. You can model a word like *help* along with a body part if your dog is sick or injured, or add another word like *hurt* or *ouch*.	• *Your dog uses words to comment or describe rather than just request.* • *Your dog has any known medical issues.* • *Your dog gestures for you to rub or scratch different body parts.*
Prepositions	*On* *Off* *Up* *Down*	We use these words frequently when talking to our dogs about getting on and off furniture, lying down or staying down, putting a collar or harness on or off, going upstairs or downstairs. These words can help your dog be more specific in their communication and share preferences about their environment.	• *Your dog combines words regularly.* • *Your dog has demonstrated the communication functions of commenting or describing.* • *You use these words regularly when talking to your dog.*

How to Choose and Introduce

With so many vocabulary options, it can be difficult to choose which you want to target next and how to structure your growth.

Remember the 2-4 rule: *It's best to introduce two to four new buttons at a time every two to four weeks.*

But now that you've introduced new words to your dog multiple times and have seen how they learned, feel free to adjust based on your experiences. If two was too few, try four at a time. If four was too many, try two at a time. If they learned four new words right away, have another two to four planned out and ready to go.

I recommend adding words that belong in the same concept groups together at the same time (e.g., *happy* and *mad*, *now* and *later*, etc.). Contrasting concepts within the same category are easiest to teach together. You can read more about this in the Activities section in this chapter, where we'll dive into how to teach each concept.

Below are some concepts that are great to introduce in the advanced stage.

Allow Your Dog to Talk More About Their Favorite Topics

By now you should have a pretty solid understanding of what your dog prefers to talk about. Hopefully they're talking about lots of different things, but there are probably a few topics that they communicate about much more than others.

Stella, for example, loves talking about the major routines of the day and where we're going. She loves pointing out deviations from our routines, elaborating on what we "should" be doing instead of what we are doing. As a herding dog, she likes knowing where her pack is and what's going on. Time concepts help her talk about the events of the day, question words enable her to ask and get the answers she needs when she's wondering what's going on, and emotions help her comment on how our actions are making her feel.

What topics does your dog prefer to talk about? What vocabulary concepts would help them communicate to their fullest potential about those topics?

Help Solve a Communication Gap You're Experiencing

Are there any times of day when it seems like your dog is trying to tell you something but doesn't have the words to? Are there words you notice yourself saying verbally often that you don't have buttons for? You can use these situations to help guide your vocabulary selections.

Add Value to Your Dog's Overall Experience

Unlike verbal speech, buttons require a significant amount of physical space. This is why we want to do our best to be efficient with the words we choose and make selections that are meaningful. To keep your dog's buttons the most functional for them, remember to pick words that you think *they* would want to say rather than words *you* want them to say.

Activities: How to Teach Advanced Concepts

Emotions: *Happy, Mad, Sad, Upset, Scared*

Emotion words represent a new communication function: *expressing feelings*. Teaching emotion words requires you to catch the emotions in action and label them, similarly to how you narrated and labeled activities as they were happening in your beginning stages of teaching words. I recommend beginning with two simple emotion words (one positive, one negative). You can get more specific by adding more later if you want. The two key times to model emotion words are when:

1. Your dog is demonstrating an emotion

Take a look back at the "Finding Your Dog's Current Communication Patterns" chart you completed in chapter 2 (see page 22). Which forms of communication did you write down for "I can tell my dog is upset when . . ." and "I can tell my dog is happy when . . ."? Are there any other patterns you've noticed since you completed this chart? If so, go ahead and add on to your answers.

When you notice any of these behaviors, label what you're seeing. By narrating your dog's emotions when they are obvious, you are setting them up to be able to express their feelings when these are less obvious to you.

Modeling Examples

- If you just played with your dog for a while and they smile at you and sit at your feet, you can model *Stella happy play. Happy play! Stella happy.*

- If you ask "Wanna go for a walk?" and your dog gets really excited, you can model *Yes happy! Stella happy walk. Happy happy.*
- If your dog asks for something, you say no, and your dog whines at you, you can model *Stella mad. Mad mad.*
- If your dog runs away whenever you get the vacuum out, you can model *Stella scared. Stella scared, scared.*

2. You or someone else is demonstrating an emotion

In chapter 11, we learned all about modeling words for different purposes, like commenting and describing. You can use those same principles here by narrating what you're feeling, too. Dogs are great at detecting different moods and responding to different emotional states. Your dog may even comment on your emotional state someday!

Modeling Examples

- If you're proud of your dog, you can model *Mom happy, Mom happy! Good Stella* while giving lots of pets and affection.
- If you're upset at something that happened, you can model *Mom mad* or *Mom upset.*
- If your child or another member of your household is noticeably happy or excited, you can model your child's name plus *happy.*
- If your child or another member of your household is crying or upset, you can model your child's name plus *upset* or *sad.*

Time: *Now, Soon, Later*

Teaching time words requires you to talk about what's happening in the present along with what you're planning to do later in the day. If your dog asks for something that will happen later on in the day, you can respond that way instead of just saying no. I recommend beginning with *now* and *later,* then adding *soon* if you feel you need it. Make sure to focus on these concepts when your dog already has a strong foundation in combining words. These aren't words that do well on their own.

Modeling **Now** Examples

All the practice you've had with narrating what's happening will pay off with this word! You can narrate what your dog is doing, what you're doing, or what is about to happen by adding *now* to your phrases.

- *Outside now* when you're about to take your dog outside
- *Eat now* as you're eating or about to feed your dog
- *Walk now* as you're getting ready to take a walk
- *Happy now* when you notice your dog is happy

Modeling **Later** Examples

You can talk about your days in the morning, telling your dog something that will happen now and something that will happen later. You can also respond to your dog's request by telling them it will happen later if it will.

- *Eat now, bye later* in the morning before feeding your dog breakfast and leaving for work. When you do leave, you can model *bye now* to put emphasis on the different time meanings.
- If your dog says *Want walk* in the middle of your day, you can say *walk later,* then model something your dog can do now instead (e.g., *play now, bed now, outside now*).
- If your dog keeps saying *eat* when she's already eaten, you can tell her *eat later*. When it's time for her next meal or a treat, you can model *eat now*.
- You can model *bye now, come later* to let your dog know that you'll be home later.

Modeling **Soon** Examples

You can add *soon* if you find your dog checking in on plans you've said are happening *later.* Stella did this frequently, so I got more detailed about her time concepts. For us, *now* represents what is happening now or in the next ten minutes, *soon* represents anything more than ten minutes to an hour, and *later* is longer than an hour. This consistency helps Stella know what to expect and anticipate how long of a wait something will be.

- *Outside soon* if you're planning to take them out when you finish eating
- *Play soon* if you're finishing up working and will play with your dog after

- *Bye soon* if you're packing up, getting ready to leave
- *Name* plus *come soon* if a family member is on their way home

Question Words: *Where, What, When, Who*

Question words allow your dog to demonstrate a new communication function: *asking questions*. By modeling question words as you ask your dog questions, you are teaching them how they can ask you questions, too. In this first stage of introducing question words, you'll notice through the examples that you'll model both the question and the answer. Modeling both the question and answer teaches your dog how these words work functionally. I recommend starting with one to two question words first and adding more if needed.

Modeling **Where?** Examples

- Before taking your dog somewhere, model *Where now?* Pause and model the answer (e.g., *Park now*), and then take your dog to the park.
- Hide one of your dog's toys. Ask *Where toy?* Then retrieve the toy for your dog and give it to them.
- Ask *Where* plus family member's name, then pause, and model the answer to where they are, or take your dog to that person if they're in a different room of the house.

Modeling **What?** Examples

- Use your buttons to say *What want?* as you ask your dog what she wants.
- Ask *What now?* Pause, then provide the answer of what you're about to do (e.g., *play now* or *bed now*).
- If your dog says *play,* you can ask *Play what?* Then pause, and provide an answer like *Play toy, play ball, play chase.*

Modeling **When?** Examples

- Ask *When* plus activity name, pause, then respond with when it's happening (e.g., *When eat?* Pause. *Eat now. When walk?* Pause. *Walk soon*).
- If your dog makes a request like *want play,* you can ask *When play?* Pause, then answer *play now* and start playing with your pup!
- Model *when* to talk through your sequences of events (e.g., *Walk when all done eat, park when all done work*).

Modeling **Who?** Examples

- Narrate your actions, your dog's actions, or other family members' actions by asking *Who* plus an activity (e.g. *eat*), pausing, then providing the answer (e.g., *Mom eat*).
- Before having a friend come over, model *Who come?* Then pause, and provide the answer of who is coming over.
- Before giving your dog lots of love and affection, model *Who love you?* Pause, then *Mom love you!* Then give scratches and belly rubs.

Body Parts: *Ears, Belly, Back, Paw, Mouth*

The names of body parts can help your dog be very specific if something is wrong. But, you don't have to wait until there's a problem to model these words. Here's how you can target them through daily activities with your dog.

Modeling Body Part Examples

- Model *love you* or *scratch* plus a body part before rubbing that part of your dog.
- If you're wiping your dog off with a towel, label the parts that you're drying verbally if you can't be by your buttons. Model with your buttons if you can.
- Model *help* plus body part name when performing standard caretaking activities (clipping nails, cleaning out ears, brushing teeth, brushing back and belly, etc.)
- If your dog has any known medical issues and is in pain or not feeling well, model the body part name along with *ouch, hurt,* or *help.*

Prepositions: *On, Off, Up, Down*

Prepositions can help your dog share preferences and observations about their environment. While I originally taught Stella *on* and *off* thinking she would communicate about if she wanted her collar on or off, she actually uses them most frequently to talk about loud sounds she's hearing or when she wants to get on a specific spot on the couch! Here's how you can teach prepositions easily.

Modeling Preposition Examples

- Model *on* or *off* when putting your dog's collar, leash, or harness on or off.
- When you have music playing or other loud noises (e.g., vacuum, blender), model *on* before turning them on and *off* right when you turn them off.
- You can invite your dog up on the couch by using *on* or *up*. If you or your dog is getting off the couch you can model *off* or *down* right after.
- If you live in a multi-level home, you can model *up* or *down* before going up or coming down the stairs. You can pair these words with names or objects to describe where they are (e.g., *Where bed? Bed up. Where Dad? Dad down*).

Summary

Advanced concepts such as times, emotions, question words, body parts and prepositions can help your dog communicate on a much deeper level. Take a look at the chart outlining advanced concepts (see pages 137–38) to learn when your dog is ready for each concept. Introduce these concepts in batches, two to four at a time, allowing two to four weeks for your dog to learn before adding more.

CHAPTER 14

Teaching Longer Phrases and Sentences

While I was on the couch sipping my morning coffee, Max, my one-year-old son, ran into the foyer and stood in front of the door. He started fussing a bit while looking up at the door handle.

Stella walked to her button board and translated exactly what was happening. *Max want outside,* she said.

Stella's ability to combine multiple words together to create phrases and short sentences has completely opened up her communication possibilities. Without words, Stella could not have shared this observation with me at all. With the ability to say single words, Stella could have said *outside,* which I likely would have interpreted as her requesting to go outside. By combining two words together, Stella could have said *want outside.* I might have gotten that she was saying what Max wanted to do, but likely still would have assumed she was telling me what she wanted to do. But by combining three words together, Stella could add all necessary elements to share her observation with me.

The stage of using longer phrases and sentences to communicate shines a light on just how much our dogs are thinking about, observing, and wanting to share with us throughout the day. It was absolutely incredible to see my dog interpreting and narrating my son's behavior similarly to how my husband or I would.

By helping your dog expand the length of their utterances and hone their communication skills, you will allow them to express a variety of thoughts, observations, opinions, and ideas to you.

When to Expect Combinations of Three or More Words

The jump from two-word phrases to multi-word phrases typically happens much faster than the time it took for your dog to go from saying single words to two-word phrases. Typically, once dogs learn how to combine words, the biggest language explosion occurs shortly after. You can expect to hear three- and four-word phrases soon when:

- Your dog uses at least a couple of two-word phrases each day
- Your dog has made a variety of two-word combinations
- Your dog repeats words or phrases when not acknowledged
- Your dog uses words for a variety of communication functions

Understanding Longer Phrases and Sentences

When dogs use multi-word phrases and short sentences to communicate, it's most similar to the *telegraphic stage* of language development, in which toddlers or young children use key functional words to convey an entire thought. For example, instead of a toddler saying, "Mom left to go to work," they might say, "Mommy bye" or "Mommy bye work." Instead of saying, "Let's take Stella for a walk," they might say, "Walk Stella" or "Take Stella walk." The telegraphic examples communicate the same thoughts as the full sentences, just without the more sophisticated grammatical markers and words.

It may take some time for you to adjust to hearing telegraphic speech and understanding the full extent of the message. As you spend more time hearing your dog talk, you'll learn their specific patterns of communication and become confident in your understanding of the messages they convey. Here are a few tips for decoding your dog's phrases:

Keep the Context in Mind

Context is key when interpreting messages from anyone (human or animal) in an earlier stage of language development. Words can be used in a variety of ways, which means the context is especially important when decoding a message. If your dog is able to provide more details with longer phrases, you'll typically have less difficulty understanding them.

Consider a Multi-Thought Message

Because your dog doesn't have the ability to use grammatical markers such as a period or a question mark, it can be difficult to distinguish between one long sentence and a couple of short phrases in a row. One of the most common examples of this is when your dog says *all done* followed by another word. Sometimes they might use *all done* to describe what they want to be done with (e.g., *all done inside*). But other times they may use *all done* plus what they want to be doing instead (e.g., *All done. Play outside* to express that they want you to stop what you're doing and go play outside with them).

Sometimes longer phrases of four to six words are actually a couple of different thoughts in one. For example, one night when we came back from swimming at the beach early and started making dinner, Stella said, *Water good* (slight pause). *No eat* (slight pause). *Play,* to communicate that she wanted to go back to swimming. Use any context clues such as increased pause time between certain words to help you decipher these longer utterances.

Your Dog's Use of All Relevant Words for a Situation

A common communication pattern for people and animals who use AAC is saying every relevant word for a situation in a row. When I worked as a speech therapist, a child might have said "All done bye off out stop finished" to let me know they wanted to be done with an activity. The child would find all the words that could signify the end of something to make sure their message was understood.

This happens with Stella and many other dogs I've worked with, too. One of my favorite examples is when Stella wanted to go out for a walk at night and said *Outside Stella Stella Stella walk come come outside* before waiting in front of the door. She used all possible words and gestures to make sure her message was received.

Activities

Recasting Revisited

In chapter 12, we learned the teaching strategy called *recasting* (see page 127). As a refresher, recasting means repeating what your dog said back to them and adding on to it. Now that your dog is using two-word phrases, you can repeat these phrases back to your dog and add an additional one to two words. This provides a model for your dog of how to make longer phrases and combine words in even more unique ways. Remember to model a variety of responses—this will help your dog learn best!

Take a look at the chart below to see examples of how to recast common phrases at this stage. Then complete your own chart, filling in common single- or two-word phrases your dog says and elaborating on how you could respond with recasts.

WHAT MY DOG SAID	WHAT I COULD SAY
Play outside	Come play outside now Stella want play outside Play ball outside
Want eat	Yes Stella eat now Stella want eat Yes Stella eat
All done. Park	Yes all done. Park now Yes all done. Play park All done. Stella want park
Come play	Mom come play Come play toy Come play now
Mad. Outside	Stella mad. Want outside Mad. Outside now Mad. No outside

Your turn!

WHAT MY DOG SAID	WHAT I COULD SAY

Dogs typically start to use combinations of three or more words more quickly than they start combining words initially. This is usually when the biggest language explosion occurs. Your dog's phrases and short sentences will be most similar to those produced during the telegraphic stage of language development in toddlers and young children.

CHAPTER 15

Conversations with Your Dog

A few minutes after my husband left to pick up our son from daycare, Stella walked to her board and said his name, Jake.

"Jake is getting Max," I replied.

Stella wagged her tail. *Where? Happy outside.*

Every afternoon when Max comes home from daycare, the four of us take a walk around the local park together. Stella looks forward to this activity every day.

"He's coming back from daycare," I said. "Then we'll all go outside together."

Stella peeked around the corner and looked to the door, waiting for Jake and Max to walk in. She returned to her buttons. *Park outside walk,* she said.

"That's right," I said. "We'll go for a walk around the park after they come home."

Even though it has been over five years since Stella started engaging in short conversations like these with me, the process never gets old. The fact that my dog and I can have a back-and-forth exchange in which she processes what's happening and what I'm saying, then shares exactly what she's thinking about, feeling, and anticipating, is mind-blowing.

In this advanced stage of learning, communication is truly a two-way street with your dog. This chapter will help you learn when to expect short conversations and what to expect from them, along with activities you can add into your interactions to promote this skill.

When to Expect Short Conversations

The majority of your dog's interactions with their buttons are likely their saying a word or phrase when they have something to say, then waiting for your response to it. Another common pattern may be your asking a general question such as "What do you want?" or issuing an opening statement such as "You can tell me" and hearing a response from your dog with buttons. These are both examples of single-turn interactions. You are each taking a turn talking, after which the conversation ends.

After your dog is very comfortable and familiar with these patterns, they may start engaging in multi-turn (back and forth three to four times) conversations. You can expect to see multi-turn conversations develop when:

- Your dog uses a variety of words and short phrases to communicate.
- Your dog responds when you give a general verbal prompt.
- Your dog whines or appears frustrated after you respond to something they said (was likely misinterpreted or is frustrated that you said no).
- Your dog communicates with words for multiple reasons beyond requesting.

What to Expect

Short conversations with your dog typically serve a few main purposes:

1 To comment on or react to a response you give
2 To provide more specific information (e.g., time, location, people, activity)
3 To adjust a message if misunderstood or unfulfilled

Conversations with your dog don't always occur at the same speed as the conversations you have in your daily life with adult human communication partners. It's important to realize that a multi-turn exchange with your dog might occur over the course of three or four minutes instead of the course of thirty seconds. Give your dog ample processing time, allow them to walk away from their buttons and return, and keep distractions at a minimum when possible. Your patience and persistence will pay off!

Also keep in mind that dialogues with learners (human or animal) in earlier stages of development don't always go as planned, and that's perfectly normal! There's a fine line between teaching different appropriate responses to questions and training a response that's conditioned. By modeling different options and allowing your dog to respond however they choose to, you are teaching different responses. Avoid repeating questions such as "What is this?" while pointing to a ball and rewarding your dog when they say *ball*. This is the equivalent of training a trick, not teaching true communication.

Conversational Patterns

The conversations to strive for are exchanges where your dog is participating twice with buttons instead of once. The two main patterns look like this:

PATTERN: *DOG-YOU-DOG*-YOU

Real-Life Example:
Stella: *Want outside*
Christina: Outside later, I'm working now.
Stella: *Mad. Play park*
Christina: I know you're mad. Play inside now, then play park later. (Get toy for Stella)

PATTERN: YOU-*DOG*-YOU-*DOG*

Real-Life Example:
Christina: What do you want, Stella?
Stella: *Play*
Christina: Play what?
Stella: *Play outside ball*

Before using buttons twice to participate in these exchanges, your dog will likely use other forms of communication such as responding with whines, barks, running to a certain location, tail wagging, huffing, etc. The above examples may look like this instead at first:

Stella: *Want outside*
Christina: Outside later, I'm working now.
Stella: (Huffs and whines)
Christina: Sorry, girl, you can play inside now. (Get toy for Stella)

Christina: What do you want, Stella?
Stella: *Play*
Christina: Play what?
Stella: (Nudges ball)

When you see this, know that your dog is especially close to using buttons twice within an exchange. Start incorporating the activities below into your interactions.

Activities

1. Narrate Your Dog's Response

When you observe your dog responding to your words with gestures, whines, or barks, label what you're seeing using your dog's buttons. This is a form of *parallel talk* (narrating your dog or someone else's actions), which we learned about in chapter 12 (see page 128). Using the same examples from above, this is what my responses could have been to Stella's whines and gestures:

EXAMPLE 1
Stella: *Want outside*
Christina: Outside later, I'm working now.
Stella: (Huffs and whines)
Christina: It looks like you're mad (press *Stella mad*). *Stella mad.*

EXAMPLE 2
Christina: What do you want, Stella?
Stella: *Play*
Christina: Play what?
Stella: (Nudges ball)
Christina: Oh, you want your ball! (press *ball*) *Play ball. Want play ball.*

Labeling what you're observing your dog communicating during your interactions will help them learn how to respond with words. When your dog is able to continue responding with words, you'll have a clearer picture of what they're trying to tell you.

2. Add a Third Turn

The best way to help your dog learn how to engage in longer conversations is by responding to your dog with their buttons. When you ask an open question or give a general verbal prompt and your dog responds, keep the exchange going! Add a third turn to the interaction. Modeling this third turn will help your dog learn how to continue adding turns as well. Here are a couple of examples:

You: What do you want?
Dog: *Eat*
You: *Yes, eat now!* (Feed your dog)

You: You can tell me.
Dog: *Walk outside*
You: *Walk soon* (Take your dog for a walk when you're ready)

3. Recast with Options

When your dog makes a request using a single word or a short phrase, you can respond by recasting (repeating and expanding) what they said with a question. Then select one of the options you provided. Here are some examples:

Dog: *Outside*
You: *What outside?* (Pause) *Walk outside?* Or *Park outside?* (Pause, then select one)

Dog: *Come come*
You: *Who come?* (Pause) *Mom come?* Or *Dad come?* (Pause, then select one)

Dog: *Want play*
You: *What want play?* (Pause) *Want play toy?* Or *Want play ball?* (Pause, then select one)

After you've spent a couple weeks incorporating this strategy into your interactions, start increasing your pause times. You can extend your first pause time to see if your dog will respond without any more cues. If they don't respond, you can ask your second question giving options. Increase your pause time again to give them a chance to respond again. Revisit the cueing hierarchy from chapter 7 (see page 76). You can work your way through that, starting with pause time and ending with a direct model if they don't respond.

Frequently Asked Questions at This Stage

I give my dog options of how to respond, but they always respond with something completely different. What should I do?

Responding to a question containing two or more options with one of those options is a more advanced language skill. Dogs can learn to do this, but it does take practice. If this skill is important to you, increase your frequency of modeling simple questions and answers. Keep your language straightforward to help your dog process and understand. Remember to use your dog's buttons as you're talking to show them how they can say what you're saying.

EXAMPLES

Want ball or want toy? (Pause) *Let's play toy!* (Grab toy and start playing)

Eat now or eat later? (Pause) *Let's eat later.*

Play outside or play inside? (Pause) *Let's play outside!* (Take your dog outside to play)

Keep in mind that your dog may not desire either of the options you provided, which is why they may not select one of them. If they respond with something completely different, you could model *No* plus the options you provided, then model *Want* plus the response your dog gave.

How do I teach my dog to answer yes or no when I ask a question?

Your dog may answer *yes* or *no* in a variety of ways other than the specific words *yes* or *no*. Pay attention to your dog's response when you ask them a question. For example, if I ask Stella "Do you want to go outside?" she will sometimes respond with *yes,* but often she responds with *outside,* confirming that yes, she does want to go outside. If she responds with something different than *outside,* that's indicative of a *no* response to me.

After you've spent some time observing your dog's response patterns, model *yes* and *no* during those times. This way you are showing your dog how they can respond in the future. Be sure to keep modeling *yes* and *no* when your dog makes comments or requests to you, too. The more they see you using these words, the more likely they are to use them themselves.

Summary

When your dog can engage in short conversations with you, communication becomes a true two-way street. Short conversations allow your dog to comment on a response you give, provide more specific information, and adjust their message if they were misunderstood. Use parallel talk and recasting to help your dog learn how to keep the conversational turns going.

CHAPTER 16

Achieving and Maintaining Proficiency

When your dog learns to use buttons to communicate, it's a lifelong skill that they can use to express their thoughts, feelings, needs, and observations to those around them. All of the work you put into the early stages of introducing buttons, modeling words, and responding to your dog will pay off exponentially for the rest of the years you'll share together.

Now, six years into my button journey with Stella, I am still thankful every day for all the work I put into teaching her early on. I truly cannot imagine our lives without Stella's being able to talk. Stella's words have reduced her anxiety and frustrations, given her a constant source of mental stimulation, and allowed her to share even the smallest observations with us. They have also given us a window into her unique mind.

If you've reached this chapter, I'm sure you have observations of your own of how words have impacted both your and your dog's lives. Take a moment to think about all the insights you've gained about your dog and how your relationship has changed now that you have a shared language. You can look back to your answers from the activities in chapter 1 (see page 15). Did you meet your goals for teaching your dog to talk? What surprised you most about your dog's journey?

Before diving into the rest of the chapter, write down any reflections here:

_____

_____

_____

_____

_____

Four Signs Your Dog's Vocabulary Is Established

At some point along your dog's button communication journey, you'll likely wonder if you have enough words or if you need to keep adding more. Below are the indicators that your dog's main vocabulary has been established:

1 Your dog has words that reflect all the main events of their days, or has created their own phrases to talk about all their routines.
2 Your dog has words to fulfill all six of the overall communication functions: requesting, protesting, commenting, describing, expressing feelings, and asking / answering questions.
3 You don't frequently experience miscommunications or gaps in communication together.
4 Your dog stops taking an interest when you add more buttons. Some dogs are knowledge seekers and will continue to want to learn as many words as you give them access to. Other dogs will revert to using a smaller subset of words if they become overwhelmed by too many buttons.

When your dog's main vocabulary is established for the foreseeable future, you can still work on more advanced skills such as responding to questions, engaging in longer conversations, and making longer phrases.

Keep in mind that throughout the course of your dog's life, you may add words here and there to represent new experiences, activities, or environments. You'll want your dog's buttons to be reflective of their life currently so they'll have the words they need to communicate effectively.

Retarget Less Used Vocabulary

If you have buttons on your dog's board that aren't used very frequently, I recommend picking one or two per week to focus on. You can either pick a concept (emotions, times, names, locations, etc.) to focus on or choose individual words that your dog doesn't say very often. Focusing on one concept or a couple of different words at a time can help you remember to target them and plan out how you're going to incorporate them into your interactions with your dog.

When Is a Dog Considered a Proficient Button Communicator?

Reaching proficiency is much more related to *how* your dog uses their buttons rather than the number of buttons on their board. For example, a dog with fifteen buttons who talks frequently throughout their days, combines multiple words together, creates their own phrases for concepts they don't have a button for, and uses their buttons to comment, express feelings, and answer questions is much more proficient than a dog who has sixty buttons on their board and uses them to make single-word requests each day.

Remember: *that the quality of communication is more important than the quantity of buttons.*

Here are the four main indicators that your dog is a proficient button communicator:

1. Your dog has used all their words intentionally.

If you've seen your dog use a word three different times in appropriate contexts, you can consider it learned. Your dog doesn't need to use all their words equally or as frequently, but a proficient button communicator has demonstrated understanding and intentionality with all of their buttons. Your dog will likely have a subset of words they use most frequently, then additional vocabulary they use as needed.

2. Your dog communicates for a variety of reasons.

A proficient button communicator has many different topics that they talk about and uses words for different communication functions. Your dog doesn't need to talk about every possible topic every day, but there should be some variety in their day-to-day communication.

3. Your dog can use their buttons with different people or in different environments.

One of the most significant markers of proficiency is your dog's ability to use their buttons when you aren't there or when the environment is different. Reaching this level can give you such peace of mind as a pet owner. You can trust that no matter what's going on or who's caring for your dog, they will be able to advocate for themselves. If they use buttons only with you, revisit chapter 10 (see page 105) to work on generalization.

4. Your dog uses their buttons both independently and when asked.

A proficient button communicator will walk up to their buttons completely on their own to say what's on their mind. They will also typically respond if you ask them what they want or tell them to use their buttons.

Maintenance Modeling

When your dog has reached proficiency, it's still important to model words for them. You don't have to model as frequently as you did in the beginning stages of learning, but the more your dog sees you using buttons in different ways, the more their skills will continue to progress and stay sharp.

To help remind yourself to use your dog's buttons, you can make a couple of maintenance modeling goals for yourself. When you practice these goals regularly, they will become habitual. Something that has worked well for me has been picking one time of the day where I consistently use Stella's buttons as I'm talking to her. The morning works well for me because I am usually the first one up in our family. I can pay attention to Stella and her words without being distracted by anything else.

Buttons That Your Dog Doesn't Use or Aren't Relevant Anymore

Due to the physical space your dog's buttons occupy, you'll want to be as efficient as possible with how many buttons your dog has available. Having a lot of buttons that aren't used spread out all over the floor can make it more challenging for your dog to use those they do want to use. Take a look at the following situations to see if it's worth revisiting which buttons you have available to them.

You Have Buttons Your Dog Has Never Used Before

If there are certain words that your dog has never interacted with, and it's been more than a few months, I recommend trying the word in a different location on your board first. You can move the button to a new empty spot and start modeling it frequently. If your dog takes more of an interest in it at that point, then keep it there. The old location was likely challenging for your dog to access for some reason. If your dog still shows no interest in that button in the new location after a few weeks of consistent modeling, you can remove the word. Sometimes it takes trial and error to determine the vocabulary set that's most beneficial for your dog. It doesn't benefit anyone to have buttons that are never used taking up space.

You Have Buttons Representing Concepts That Aren't Relevant Anymore

When life changes occur (losing a pet, moving, changing routines), you may have words that don't reflect your daily life anymore. I recommend following your dog's lead with removing these buttons. For example, when we moved from a beach neighborhood in San Diego to the Chicago suburbs, *beach* was no longer relevant for us. I did not remove Stella's *beach* button, as I wanted to know if she was still thinking about it. For weeks after our move she still talked about the beach. She would ask *Where beach?* or say *Want beach* or *Love you beach*. If I had removed the *beach* button, she wouldn't have been able to express any of these thoughts to me. When winter hit, Stella stopped talking about the beach altogether, probably because we had never visited a beach in such cold temperatures! But to my surprise, when spring came around, Stella started asking about the beach again. We began using *beach* to describe the nearby river and lakefronts we would take her to. Her definition of *beach* changed with the changing circumstances.

If you're going through a move or don't visit people or places that you previously visited before, I recommend keeping the word available until your dog no longer uses it anymore. It would be jarring for your dog to be thinking about or remembering a concept, then suddenly not have the ability to communicate about it. If your dog does stop using a word, you can remove the button and keep the space empty for a couple of weeks before programming a new word into it.

Activities

1. Create Maintenance Modeling Goals for Yourself

Example Goals

1   I will use my dog's buttons at least twice per day while I'm talking to or responding to them.
2   I will recast (repeat and expand) on at least one of my dog's phrases each day.

Your turn!

1   _____.
2   _____.

2. Word / Concept of the Week

Pick a word or concept each week to retarget. Treat this word or concept like you're introducing it for the first time. This means increasing your modeling to multiple times each day, providing more pause time and other cues, and using it in a variety of different contexts. See modeling ideas below for different concepts that you might be retargeting:

- *Emotions:* Talk about how you're feeling, what emotions your dog is demonstrating before and after activities, or emotions another family member is displaying.
- *Times:* When your dog makes a request, recast by adding *now, soon,* or *later,* depending on when it's happening, and narrate your actions paired with *now* and your dog's actions paired with *now.*
- *Names:* Narrate your actions, your dog's actions, and the actions of others in your household. Talk about who you're going to visit. Ask your dog who they want to play with or go for a walk with.
- *Locations:* Talk about where you're going before you leave, then com-

ment on the experience when you return home. Ask your dog "Where?" when she says she wants to play or go out.

- *Objects:* Hide your dog's toys or other favorite things and look for them together. Model the word for the object as you're looking for it and when you find it.

Summary

When your dog uses all their words independently and achieves all the markers of proficiency, their foundational vocabulary is likely established. You can continue adding words throughout their lifespan as new situations arise. Make sure to keep up maintenance modeling so your dog's skills stay sharp.

CONCLUSION

When I worked as a speech therapist, I had the following quote taped on the wall above my desk.

The limits of my language mean the limits of my world.

—*Ludwig Wittgenstein*

This quote reminds me that language and communication connect us all and open up our worlds. Language gives us the ability to connect to both loved ones and strangers by sharing our experiences, expressing our minds with one another, and processing the world around us. My hope is that this guidebook has helped open up a new world of communication between you and your dog, has connected you two together in a deeper way, and has shed light on your dog's unique mind and intelligence. Being able to share a language with another species is an incredible privilege.

Any progress that you've made throughout your button communication journey should be celebrated! Whether you learned how to respond to your dog's current forms of communication, taught your dog to say a few basic words, or are having short conversations with your pup every day, I'm confident that your dedication to communication will change your dog's life for the better.

I am finishing this manuscript on the sixth anniversary of Stella's saying her very first word, *outside*. Six years ago today, I was filled with excitement, optimism, and wonder as I watched Stella so deliberately tell me she had to go to the bathroom by using her button for the first time. I couldn't wait to see what else she would learn to say and how her communication would progress. Today I'm filled with the same excitement, optimism, and wonder as I think about what *you* will discover with your dog and where this talking dog movement will go next. There is so much left to learn about what dogs are capable of, and *you* have the opportunity to be part of these discoveries.

Now that you've read and worked through the three stages of learning, you are well-equipped to teach any concept that comes your way. *Your Dog Can Talk* was designed to help you blossom into an informed teacher, ready to make your own decisions and apply these principles to unique words or situations. I encourage you to keep observing your dog's communication, using their buttons to talk to them, and giving them opportunities to say new words.

If this guidebook has helped your dog learn to talk, share your story with others! The more people see what's possible from their pets, the greater the changes we can make as a society in how we view and treat animals who share our homes with us. Take videos of your dog talking, write a blog or social media post, or invite your friends over to hear what your dog has to say. By teaching your own dog to talk, you are playing an important role in this new era of interspecies communication and are showing the world that everyone deserves a voice.

Thank you so much for allowing me to be a part of your dog's button communication journey. It brings me such joy to see pet parents around the world teaching their dogs to talk, and I'm truly honored to have played a part in this experience for you.

In the words of Stella, *All done. Love you. Bye.*

APPENDIX: BUTTON COMMUNICATION FUNCTIONS

The table below shows the six overall functions of communication, the stage(s) in which you can expect to observe each stage, and example utterances.

FUNCTION	STAGE(S)	EXAMPLES
Requesting	Beginner–Advanced	Beginner: *Outside* Intermediate: *Want outside* Advanced: *Come outside now*
Protesting	Intermediate–Advanced	Intermediate: *All done, no* when your dog doesn't want to do something Advanced: *Sound off* when your dog hears a loud sound such as a blender or vacuum
Describing	Intermediate–Advanced	Intermediate: *Water, water outside* when your dog sees rain outside Advanced: *Mom bye now* when your dog sees you getting ready to leave
Commenting	Intermediate–Advanced	Intermediate: *Good eat* after having an especially yummy treat Advanced: *Stella happy play* after a fun play session, *Mad eat now* when dinner has been delayed
Asking / Answering Questions	Advanced	Asking questions: *Where ball? Where Mom?* Answering Questions: *Yes want, Want play outside*
Expressing Feelings	Advanced	*All done happy outside* when you're done with work for the day, *Mad eat now* when dinner has been delayed

GLOSSARY

2-4 Rule: It's best to introduce two to four new buttons at a time every two to four weeks.

Augmentative and alternative communication (AAC): All forms of communication other than verbal speech that help individuals communicate to their fullest potential. AAC is an area of speech-language pathology typically used to help people with verbal speech challenges communicate.

Babbling: Pressing different buttons in a row for exploratory purposes.

Button communication: A form of AAC created for dogs, cats, and other domestic animals to be able to say words.

Core words: "A small set of simple words that are used frequently and across contexts." Core words are typically verbs, adjectives, prepositions, conjunctions, and pronouns, and make up the majority of what we say.

Cues: Helpful reminders you can give your dog as they're learning.

Exploratory learner: A learner who learns primarily from exploring their buttons and seeing how their communication partner responds.

Expressive language: An individual's ability to express thoughts, wants, needs, and ideas.

Fringe words: "Words specific to a topic, individual, or environment." Fringe words are mostly nouns and proper nouns.

Generalization: The ability to demonstrate a skill in an environment different from the one a learner was taught in.

The Hunger for Words Method: A systematic approach to teaching dogs to communicate with buttons, derived from principles of augmentative communication, early language development, and dog cognition.

Intermediate words: Offer potential for combining and can be used for purposes other than requesting.

Interspecies communication: Communication between different species of animals or between humans and animals.

Joint attention: An important language developmental milestone in which the learner uses their eye gaze, gestures, or body language to direct your attention to an object.

Language: "A system of conventional spoken, manual (signed), or written symbols by means of which beings express themselves."

Levels of support: The amount of assistance you're giving your dog as you're teaching. Levels of support are determined by the types of cues you provide

Modeling: Using your dog's buttons in the right contexts to talk about what's happening around them.

Motor plan / Motor learning: The process in which repeated actions become automatic through muscle memory.

Observant learner: A learner who learns mostly through watching their humans use the buttons. Their interest in using the buttons themselves increases over time after observing patterns.

Parallel talk: A type of narration in which you describe what someone else is doing.

Parentese: Simple language that parents use to talk to their infant, often at a slower rate and higher pitch than their typical speech.

Receptive language: An individual's language comprehension.

Self-talk: A type of narration in which you describe what you're doing.

Strengths-based teaching: "A process for identifying strengths involving the recognition and acknowledgment of preferences, abilities, and passions."

ACKNOWLEDGMENTS

This book could not have been possible without the tremendous support I received from my family. To my husband, Jake, thank you for running nearly all parts of our household while I was eight months pregnant and finishing this book. The way you took care of Max, Stella, our home, and me during this time was incredible. You are the biggest supporter of my dreams.

To my parents, Brian and Laura Hunger, and to my in-laws, Rusty and Marilyn McConkey, thank you for all the times you watched Max so I could write longer. I am so grateful for your help!

To my great friend Grace Stevens, thank you for reading my manuscript drafts and providing your thoughtful feedback. I feel so lucky to have you in my life personally and professionally!

To my literary agent, Ryan Harbage, and the team at Ten Speed Press, thank you for making this book become a reality. I've spent years envisioning a training book and am thrilled that it now exists to help pet parents around the world.

To all my training clients, thank you so much for giving me the opportunity to work with you and learn from your experiences. Your stories, feedback, and questions all impacted the development of this book and inspired me to keep creating resources.

Finally, thank you to Stella. None of this would have been possible without you and your voice. You have inspired an entirely new field of interspecies communication and have paved the way for dogs all around the world to share their voices too. Thank you for showing the world what dogs are capable of. We love you so much!

NOTES

Chapter 1: Why Button Training?

2   **dogs do understand the button words:** A.P.M. Bastos, A. Evenson, P. M. Wood, et al., "How Do Soundboard-Trained Dogs Respond to Human Button Presses? An Investigation into Word Comprehension," *PLOS One* 19, no. 8 (2024): e0307189. https://doi.org/10.1371/journal .pone.0307189.

2   **are creating meaningful, intentional word combinations:** A.P.M. Bastos, Z. N. Houghton, L. Naranjo, et al., "Soundboard-Trained Dogs Produce Nonaccidental, Non-Random, and Non-Imitative Two-Button Combinations," *Science Reports* 14, 28771 (2024), https://doi.org/10.1038/s41598-024-79517-6.

9   **cognitive capabilities close to those of a human child:** "Smarter Than You Think: Canine Researcher Puts Dogs' Intelligence on Par with 2-Year-Old Human," American Psychological Association press release 2009, accessed April 18, 2024, https://www.apa.org/news/press/ releases/2009/08/dogs-think.

9   **over 1,000 different toys:** John W. Pilley and Alliston K. Reid, "Border Collie Comprehends Object Names as Verbal Referents," *Behavioural Processes* 86, no. 2 (2011): 184–95, doi: 10.1016/j.beproc.2010.11.007.

9   **what they meant when combined together:** John W. Pilley, "Border Collie Comprehends Sentences Containing a Prepositional Object, Verb, and Direct Object," *Learning and Motivation* 44, no. 4 (2013): 229–40, doi: 10.1016/j.lmot.2013.02.003.

11   **Anxiety and frustration affect:** M. Salonen, S. Sulkama, S. Mikkola, et al., "Prevalence, Comorbidity, and Breed Differences in Canine Anxiety in 13,700 Finnish Pet Dogs," *Science Reports* 10, 2962 (2020), https://doi.org/10.1038/s41598-020-59837-z.

12   **Providing dogs with more choices:** Gemma Johnstone, "Empower Your Dog by Offering Them More Choices and Autonomy," *American Kennel Club,* accessed September 10, 2024, https://www.akc.org/expert-advice/training/offer-dog-more-choices-and-autonomy/#:~:text=Training%20Without%20Force,they%20picked%2C%E2%80%9D%20suggests%20Bloom.

Chapter 2: Learning Your Dog's Language

20   **verbal words that develop later:** Jana M. Iverson and Susan Goldin-Meadow, "Gesture Paves the Way for Language Development," *Psychological Science* 16, no. 5 (2005): 367–71, doi: 10.1111/j.0956-7976.2005.01542.x.

Chapter 3: Selecting Beginning Words

30   **"a small set of simple words":** "Core Words," Fluent AAC, no date, accessed April 29, 2024, https://www.fluentaac.com/core-words.

31   **80 percent of what we say:** Frontiers, "Most Adults Know More Than 42,000 Words," *ScienceDaily*, August 16, 2016, www.sciencedaily.com/releases/2016/08/160816111017.htm.

Chapter 4: Setting Up Your Buttons

40   **"Conscious thought is no longer needed":** John Halloran and Cindy Halloran, "LAMP: Language Acquisition Through Motor Planning," 2006, the Center for AAC & Autism, www.aacandautism.com.

Chapter 5: Modeling Language

49   **"four times more likely":** Brian Hare and Vanessa Woods, *The Genius of Dogs: How Dogs Are Smarter Than You Think* (New York: Dutton, 2013).

52   **language development outcomes for the baby:** Nairán Ramírez-Esparza, Adrián García-Sierra, and Patricia K. Kuhl, "Look Who's Talking NOW! Parentese Speech, Social Context, and Language Development Across Time," *Frontiers in Psychology* 8 (2017): 1008, doi: 10.3389/fpsyg.2017.01008, https://www.ncbi.nlm.nih.gov/pmc/articles/PMC5477750/.

Chapter 10: Generalizing Skills

105 **"practicing with your dog":** Pat Miller, "Dog Trainers Use of Generalizing a Behavior," *Whole Dog Journal,* September 11, 2008; updated April 24, 2023, https://www.whole-dog-journal.com/training/dog-trainers-use-of-generalizing-a-behavior/.

Chapter 11: Using Words for Different Reasons

114 *requesting, protesting, describing:* David R. Beukelman and Pat Mirenda, *Augmentative and Alternative Communication: Supporting Children and Adults with Complex Communication Needs,* 4th ed. (Baltimore: Paul H. Brookes Publishing Co., 2012).

Chapter 14: Teaching Longer Phrases and Sentences

148 **key functional words to convey:** American Psychological Association, "Telegraphic Speech," *APA Dictionary of Psychology,* no date, accessed April 29, 2024, https://dictionary.apa.org/telegraphic-speech.

Glossary

175 **"A small set of simple words":** "Core Words," Fluent AAC, no date, accessed April 29, 2024, https://www.fluentaac.com/core-words.

175 **"Words specific to a topic":** "What Are Fringe Words?" Communication Community, July 18, 2020, https://www.communicationcommunity.com/what-are-fringe-words/.

176 **"A system of conventional spoken":** K. Turcios, "What Is Language?" Stillman Translations, no date, accessed April 10, 2024, https://www.stillmantranslations.com/language-functions-of-language-definition-of-language-translations/.

176 **"A process for identifying strengths":** Jim Paterson, "New Focus on Strength-Based Learning," NEA Today, June 9, 2022, https://www.nea.org/nea-today/all-news-articles/new-focus-strength-based-learning.